VALUE EXPLORATION THROUGH ROLE PLAYING

VALUE EXPLORATION THROUGH ROLE PLAYING

Practical Strategies for Use in the Classroom

Robert C. Hawley

HART PUBLISHING COMPANY, INC.
NEW YORK CITY

CONTENTS

To Mary Coit Hawley

FOREWORD

Like most teachers, I appreciate a good class discussion with active participation by many of the students. Therefore, I was delighted to discover role playing as a sure-fire way to trigger lively discussion and significant contributions from an unusually large portion of the class. Role playing produces this vitality because it spotlights human interaction; that is, it brings out the values implicit in behavior so that these values may be the subject of concrete inquiry. A role play of only one to five minutes can generate a multitude of specific data for analysis. Students can pick up on different aspects of the interaction—communicating, seeking alternatives, differentiating conflicts, identifying and solving problems, forecasting consequences. All this arises naturally out of the exchange.

It's unfortunate that teachers don't use role playing more often. In my first fourteen years of teaching (mostly in junior high schools), I never used role playing, although I was familiar with the term and thought that I understood what it was all about. Perhaps I avoided role playing because I didn't want to waste my precious class time in "playing" when we could be having a serious discussion. Yet those "serious discussions" were games in themselves—"Guess What I'm Thinking Of" games in which the students would try to match answers to my questions and thus patch together what amounted to a thinly veiled lecture.

Moreover, while the class was nominally engaged in an "open discussion," I did 80 to 90 percent of the talking, and a group of three or four of the "best" students took up nearly all of what little time remained.

A second reason that some teachers may decline to use role playing is that they fear the possibilities of unleashing emotional forces which they feel inadequate to deal with. Certainly role playing can generate strong feelings; but I believe that these feelings are probably less dangerous than the strong feelings which are developed at a basketball game, or when report cards come out, or when a student suddenly feels rejected by his classmates or his teacher. Furthermore, since feelings are one of the legitimate areas of investigation for the role-playing class, it is likely that they can be dealt with in a satisfactory manner, especially with the guidelines provided in this book.

Besides their not wanting to "waste" time in "play," and their fear of the emotional content, it is sometimes said that teachers disdain role playing because they are afraid to move into an area where they do not have the same tight control over the path of the discussion as they have in a conventional class setting. I tend to discount this reason. Few of the teachers I have known are timid persons; rather, the great majority of them are naturally active, forceful people, willing to take risks where there is a reasonable chance of success. A much more likely reason for teachers' reluctance to engage in role playing is simply that they don't know how to get started, or what procedures might be most effective.

And here we have the reason for this book—to give teachers the specific know-how they need to incorporate role playing into their repertoire of teaching techniques. For role playing is not an end in itself; it is just one means in the service of good teaching, teaching which promotes the growth of each learner.

Role playing is so rich with learning opportunities for both the participants and the observers that the level of involvement is unusually high. Different students can center on interests that are particularly germane to them. For instance, one student may be discovering new alternatives in thought and action for a particular concern; a second student may be learning new approaches to problem-solving; a third may be involved in observing and analyzing the variety of human interactions that are taking place; and a fourth may be "stepping into another person's shoes," learning to empathize and thus grow in human understanding

—all through the same role play. Thus, by meeting a variety of individual needs simultaneously, role playing reaches many students at their moment of readiness for learning.

There are two additional points to recommend the use of role play:

1. Students are growing ever more discontent with their passive role in the learning process (i.e., as recipients of knowledge imparted by teacher, textbooks, etc.). Role playing is one teaching method that involves students actively in the learning process, both in simulated interactions and in determining what path to take in the discussions that follow the role play.

2. Role playing is a common and natural human activity, not just another artificial structure limited to the classroom. Young children regularly initiate role-playing situations among themselves, and they often engage in lengthy role plays. My preschool-aged daughter and her friends often spend long afternoons in "Baby and Mother and Doctor," or "Mother and Father and Baby," etc. For older children, there are "Cops and Robbers," "Cowboys and Indians," "Astronauts," and the like. And, as Eric Berne has indicated in *Games People Play* (Grove Press, 1968), adults are adept at such role

plays as "Top Dog, Under Dog," "Wooden Leg," "Uproar," and others.

I am indebted to Dr. Jeffrey W. Eiseman of the University of Massachusetts for introducing me to role playing. His innovative approaches to teaching have had a substantial influence on this book. I am also indebted to the many groups and classes which have allowed me to experiment unabashedly with them. And finally, I owe a debt of gratitude to my wife, Dr. Isabel L. Hawley, who put aside the book that she is writing to keep domestic chaos from my study door.

Chapter One

DECISIONS: AN OPEN-CHAIR ROLE PLAY

The class is seated in a circle. In the center of the circle are two empty chairs facing each other. A paper face is taped to the back of each chair; one is labeled "Sue," the other, "Dad." Sitting on the floor at the foot of Sue's chair are three students who will speak for Sue. Three more students sit at the foot of Dad's chair to speak for Dad.

The teacher, who is seated among the students on the circumference of the circle, reviews the confrontation situation which the class has just invented:[1]

"Sue is a fifteen-year-old girl. She's been invited to go to the big rock concert at the State University, which is ninety miles away, by Jim, the boy she met last summer. Jim is nineteen and a sophomore at the University. Since the University is so far away, Sue has arranged to spend the night with Jim's sister, Ann, who is a freshman there.

"I'm going to time the role play, and I will cut it at the end of five minutes or, more likely, before.

But in any case, it won't last more than five minutes.
"You can start now."

[In the following dialogue, any of the three students sitting by Sue's chair may speak for Sue, while any of the other three may speak for Dad.]

SUE: Hi, Dad.

DAD: Oh, hi there, Sue.

SUE: Say, Dad, there's something I've been meaning to ask you.

DAD: Go ahead, Sue. You know I'm always glad to have you come to me about anything, anything at all.

SUE: Well, Dad, you remember Jim, don't you? That nice boy I met last summer at the beach?

DAD: Let me see—Jim—Jim. Oh, yes, the one with the long hair and the motorcycle?

SUE: Yeah, well he's sold the motorcycle now; he needed money for college.

DAD: Oh, well . . . well, what about him?

SUE: You see, there's this great concert at the University—

DAD: What kind of a concert?

SUE: Well, the Steam Machine is going to be there—a great group, I'm sure you've heard me play their records. And Little Joey and Funk will be there, and some others, too. Dad, *everybody's* going to be there.

DAD: Now wait a minute. Did you say at the University? That's ninety miles away.

SUE: We've got that all worked out. I can drive up with some of the kids that are going from here and then spend the night with Ann.

DAD: Ann? Who's Ann?

SUE: That's Jim's sister, she's a freshman. She lives in the dorm right on campus.

DAD: Now wait a minute, Sue. I know about those blasts, the drinking and the marijuana. And I've heard about what goes on in the dorms there. Besides, that's for college-age. How old are you?

SUE: Dad, I'm almost sixteen. I'm not a little girl any more.

TEACHER: Cut! Thank you. Comments?

STUDENT: Boy, just like my father! Whatever it is, you can't do it because you're too young.

SECOND STUDENT: Well, he really hasn't said "no" yet. I think that if Sue plays her cards right, she's still got a chance.

THIRD STUDENT: Nah! She blew her chance when she let on that she had her plan all worked out, sort of behind her father's back.

FOURTH STUDENT: Well, my parents are different, they want me to make my own plans and then just come to them for approval.

FIFTH STUDENT: I think the whole situation is unrealistic. Sue ought to have started dropping hints about the concert weeks ago so that it didn't come as such a big surprise.

The lively discussion continues—because it is based on events which have just occurred, and because the Sue-Dad situation is grounded in the experience of the students. For these reasons, the discussion is specific, relevant, and probing, seldom characterized by the vague generalizations which often dominate classroom discussions.

This brief role play lasted less than three minutes, yet it provided the material for a lively half-hour discussion which included the following topics:

1. *The perceived relationship between father and daughter, especially in the light of the father's statement that he is always glad to have Sue come to him with any matter.* Did Dad's subsequent actions reflect his assertion? Is it really wise, or even safe, to share problems with one's parents? Are there some things that parents would really rather not know about? Do parents put up barriers to prevent their children from being open with them? Do young people put up barriers which prevent them from being open with their parents? What changes could Sue make in her behavior to let Dad know that she wanted to be more open to him (if she wanted to be)?

2. *Sue's and Dad's attempts to manipulate each other while jockeying for a more favorable po-*

sition. What is the nature of the power struggle in this relationship and what is the currency of power —affection, face, money, good will, etc?

3. *The hidden messages that pass between them*. What underlies Dad's reference to Jim as having long hair and a motorcycle? Why does Sue point out that Jim needs money for college?

4. *Peer pressure*. Sue says that *everybody* is going to be at the concert. Is it possible to go to a concert where "everybody" is smoking marijuana and not smoke it yourself?

5. *Drugs, promiscuity, alcohol, and other ugly heads to rear*. Have decisions on these matters already been made by the age of fifteen, thus making discussion the equivalent of "beating a dead horse" (as one girl put it)? Or do these matters require an ongoing reevaluation as situations change? What hard information is needed to make decisions in these areas? To what degree are the laws of the land important in making such decisions (since a violation of statutory law might be involved)?

6. *Generating alternatives and testing probable consequences of each*. In what other ways might Sue bring the subject to Dad? What would be his probable responses to each way? Are there

alternative arrangements that could be made to deal with Dad's concerns yet still satisfy Sue's wishes? What about alternatives to the concert itself—are there other ways for Sue and Jim to see each other that will be more acceptable to Dad?

7.   *Comparisons of life styles.* Extrapolating from the confrontation between Sue and Dad, how does a similar experience of one member of the class compare with the experiences of others in the class? What advantages and disadvantages do students perceive in their own situations and in the situations of their classmates?

8.   *Issues of trust, responsibility, authority, control and freedom.* Maturation and rites of passage—when does one come of age?

9.   *Forecasting probable outcomes.* From what you have seen of the role play thus far, do you think that Dad will allow Sue to go? How will this discussion between them end—with a shouting match, or someone in tears, or with a polite "thank you"? Or some other way? What specific behaviors of Dad and Sue lead you to your prediction?

10.   *Awareness of true end goals of behavior.* Which is more important to Sue—Jim or the concert, or some other factor?

Although no definitive general consensus has been reached by the end of the half-hour, enough issues have been discussed in depth so that the class can be more fully aware of the facets of interaction which go into making a decision. At this point, the teacher asks the students to refocus on Sue's problem in the following way:

TEACHER: Now let's go back to the beginning again. What could Sue do to bring about a no-lose decision—a decision in which neither Sue nor Dad will feel that he or she has lost face with the other? I don't want you to think only about the outcome— that is, whether Sue goes to the concert or not—but rather to give some thought to *how* the decision is made. It may be, for instance, that the best course of action is for Sue not to go to the concert. We're not trying to work Dad into a corner so that he has to say Yes, and we're not building a case for Dad so that he can say No with justification. What I'd like us to work on is the *process* that Sue and Dad use in making the decision, so that whatever the outcome, neither Sue nor Dad feels manipulated, neither feels a loss in self-respect, and neither has a lingering resentment toward the other.

STUDENT: Do you mean a kind of compromise?

TEACHER: Well, the final decision could be some kind of compromise, but I don't know the answer. If I did, I'd be telling you instead of asking you.

Let's consider what things can be done to keep the focus on the problem at hand: whether or not Sue should go to the concert. It is all too easy in a confrontation like this to shift from the conflict to the personalities involved. For instance, when Dad asks how old Sue is, he's beginning to shift the ground to an attack on Sue and her trustworthiness. Now he may be justified in having doubts about how Sue will act in this situation because of her age; but to ask the question "How old are you?"— a purely rhetorical question, since he knows the answer perfectly well—is like waving a red flag in her face. This prompts Sue to raise her defenses; she tries to meet Dad's challenge by building herself up, saying that she's "almost sixteen."

A more dramatic example of how the ground of discussion can shift would be if Sue had said, "You *never* trust me!" That clearly directs the focus away from the problem and toward the personality of Dad. Now Dad must defend himself from this attack. He will dredge up past transgressions, real or imagined, as justification for "never trusting" Sue, or he will counterattack by pointing out weaknesses in *her* personality. And thus the conflict escalates into an interpersonal battle where someone —probably both of them—will lose.

Now, what sorts of things can Sue do or say to bring about a no-lose decision?

STUDENT: Well, she could start off by saying that she has a problem and wants his help in figuring out what to do.

TEACHER: Okay. That's a useful approach, so long as the request is genuine. On the other hand, if Sue's really got only one answer in mind, and she's trying to manipulate Dad around to that answer, then at some point he's likely to feel used, and he's bound to resent that.

SECOND STUDENT: They could try to work out some alternative arrangement that would eliminate Dad's objections. Maybe if Dad drove Sue to the concert, or something like that.

THIRD STUDENT: That would never work! What would be the point of going if Dad will be there? And besides, he'd never drive ninety miles just so Sue could be with Jim.

TEACHER: Well, that may be. We seem to be clarifying Sue's goals: one goal may be to get away from Dad, another to be with Jim. The idea of Dad's driving Sue to the University might be an unrealistic solution for some Sues and some Dads, but for others it might work out nicely. The more alternatives we can come up with, even ones that seem to be unrealistic, the more likely we are to find one that will be acceptable. People often operate within a fairly narrow range of behaviors because they don't think of possible alternatives. For instance, Sue may think that her father would never consent to drive that distance, while Dad might, in fact, be perfectly willing and even pleased to do it.

STUDENT: Another alternative would be for Jim to come to Sue's house, and they could listen to her stereo. They could even buy some new records with the money they saved.

TEACHER: That's right. If the main goal is for them to see each other, then that could work.

STUDENT: I'd like to get back to the question of age. That always seems to come up in our house —"You can't do that. You're too young." The question really isn't how old Sue is as much as how responsible she is, how much she can be trusted to do the right thing on her own. I resent being classed as a fifteen-year-old. I want to be judged on the basis of being me.

TEACHER: Here we're beginning to define Dad's problem—that is, how can he determine the degree of Sue's responsibility and trustworthiness in this particular situation? But it's important to avoid drifting away into vague generalities. What does Dad mean by trust? What would he consider responsible behavior or irresponsible behavior? For instance, would Dad consider Sue irresponsible if she drank a can of beer? Or would it be two cans? What if she smoked a joint? Would that be an example of something that Dad would consider irresponsible? Or, suppose she went riding in an automobile with someone who was high on grass?

STUDENT: Well, she might not have any choice about that. I mean if they were way out in the country somewhere and it was her only way to get back—

TEACHER: This might be what Dad would worry about; he could have a real concern for his daughter's physical safety. At some point, Sue might lose control of her situation: her options could close down on her so that she would be forced into a decision that she might later regret.

STUDENT: But that could happen to someone much older, too.

TEACHER: That's right. Being "responsible" isn't purely a function of age. It involves the ability to forecast events and make decisions on the basis of an awareness of the long-range consequences. So a girl of fifteen who was highly aware of the possible long-range consequences in a given situation might make a better decision than a nineteen-year-old girl who was not aware of the possible consequences. On the other hand, one generally becomes aware of possible consequences through experience, and the nineteen-year-old girl would have four more years of experience than the fifteen-year-old.

Role playing is one way of examining the possible consequences of a decision. Another time, we might role play what would happen at the concert, for instance.

The power of role play and discussion comes from the fact that the three facets of decision making—the interpersonal, the rational, and the emotional—are being worked on at the same time. Since almost every personal decision affects other people and is influenced by other people, decision making can be seen as an interpersonal process. And insofar as the level of information at one's grasp helps to shape the decision, and the decision can be affected by the application of logic and reasoning, decision making can be seen as a rational process. And last, insofar as the decision is based on the strength of the desires and wishes of the one who makes the decision, decision making can be seen as an emotional process.

Student involvement in role play is high because the material is generated by the students directly out of their own concerns. Because there are no wrong answers, the risk involved in participation is low, and the discussion is less likely to be subverted by the traditional classroom games of "Guess What the Teacher's Thinking Of" or "Can You Top This?"

Moreover, the teacher can use role play to discover which areas are of special interest to students, and to evaluate the level of information or misinformation present in the class. These findings enable the teacher to set up further learning experiences that will address the interests of students and at the same time provide relevant information.

Decisions Role Play, Step by Step

Let's look closely at the procedure that the teacher used in setting up and conducting the role play of Sue and Dad (the procedure is similar for all Decisions Role Plays):

1. The teacher orients the students to the subject matter, saying something like the following:

"Today we're going to look at the process of deciding. We'll identify some of the factors which are involved in making a decision, and we'll try to come up with some ideas about how we can make more effective decisions about the things that are important to us.

"To get started, reflect over the past year and try to think of the most important decision you have had to face. Then write it down on a slip of paper—just for yourself. You won't have to show your paper to anyone. But after class, you might want to look at the decision you wrote down, and see whether you view that decision at all differently."

2.   The teacher elicits topics of concern from the class, using the open-chair technique to reduce the risk. He places an empty chair at the front of the room, and tapes a paper face to its back. Then he says:

"This is Sue.[2] Sue is a girl who is just about your age and lives around here. Let's set up a role-playing situation in which Sue is to face a decision of some kind. (Next time we'll take Dan,[2] and a decision of his.)

"I'd like you to brainstorm—that is, shoot out as many ideas as come to you—for four minutes on all the decisions that Sue is likely to face in the next year of her life. The rules of brainstorming are simple: all ideas are welcome, and the more ideas the better, even wild ones. Build on one another's ideas. I'll write the ideas on the board as you call them out."

The rules of brainstorming that the teacher should keep in mind are six:

1.   No negative evaluation of any idea during the brainstorming period.

2.   Work for quantity.

3.   Zany, far-out ideas are encouraged.

4.   Piggy-back or springboard off one

another's ideas—if someone's idea prompts an idea in your head, then share it.

5. Write down each idea.

6. Set a time limit for the brainstorming session and adhere to it.

The brainstormed list of decisions that Sue is likely to face in the next year of her life (four minute model):

1. Dyeing hair.

2. Whom to go out with.

3. Nose surgery.

4. Mother's Day gift.

5. Try out for play.

6. Have intercourse.

7. Smoke dope.

8. Leave home.

9. How to dress.

10. Parting of hair.

11. Dates.

12. How to deal with parents.

13. Getting a job.

14. Diet.

15. Marriage.

16. Addict of Vivarin or Midol.

17. What courses to take.

18. Smoke cigarettes.

19. Nail polish.

20. What to buy for Christmas.

21. Whether to go to a bar.

22. Join the tennis team.

23. Tell her parents about VD.

24. Driving.

25. Acne.

26. Cut hair.

27. Cut classes.

28. Ears pierced.

29. Braces.

30. College.

31. Follow the crowd.

32. Religion.

33. Lacrosse practice.

34. Abortion.

3. The teacher sets up the role-play situation by taking nominations from the brainstorming list for a decision that the students would like to pursue. Let us say that, by a show of hands, item number 12, "How to deal with parents," is selected. Next the teacher tells the class:

"Develop a situation for role playing, using the following formula: Sue is about to confront one other person with a specific demand or request. That is, she could be asking the person or telling the person about some specific action to be taken. Who is that other person, where are they, and what is the specific action that she is asking or telling about?"

Let's say that the class develops the situation involving Sue and Dad and the concert with Jim.

4. Have the class move into the role-playing format, setting up the circle of chairs with the open chairs in the center. *Point out that no one will be asked to sit in the chairs.* (This format can look very threatening if students think that they might have to sit out there in the middle with all of their peers observing them.) Then call for volunteers: "I would like three volunteers to speak for Sue and three volunteers to speak for Dad, in a short role play that will last no more than five minutes. It's all right for boys to volunteer for Sue and girls for Dad."

NOTE: At this point, some teachers may wonder what to do if no one volunteers. In fact, this almost never happens. But if, after a long and embarrassing silence (at least twenty seconds) no volunteers are forthcoming, the teacher can simply divide the circle in half and assign one half to the role of Sue and the other half to the role of Dad.

5.   The volunteers sit on the floor[3] beside the chair that they are speaking for, and the role play is ready to begin. At this point, the role players might ask the teacher if they should get together and decide on a specific approach in order to present a consistent character. The teacher should answer that there is no need to get together, because there is no need for a character to be consistent.

The role players may also ask for clarification as to the background of the situation to be enacted. The teacher should avoid the temptation to fill in additional information, because background material tends to interfere with the immediacy and spontaneity of the role play. When the players are continually thinking about whether what they intend to say is consistent with the background as they remember it, they become inhibited; they become caught up with creating a character rather than living a part.

6.   In conducting the role play itself, setting

a time limit is an important risk-reducing factor. The teacher should clearly indicate that he is going to cut in at the end of a specific period of time (usually four or five minutes), or before. Some students are more likely to volunteer if they know that their risk will be limited to a short period of time. The assurance that the teacher will cut the role play also releases players from the compulsion to build exit lines into their scripts.

To begin the role play, the teacher should simply say, "Begin." He should not direct one party or the other to initiate the conversation, nor should he suggest what the opening line should be. To end the role play the teacher should shout, "Cut!" at the end of the given time, regardless of what's going on in the role play. Don't wait for an appropriate moment to break in; there is likely never to be one.

During the role play, comments or suggestions from the outside circle should not necessarily be discouraged unless such comments disrupt the situation or disturb the players. If the role players seem unsure as to how to proceed, the teacher can call for suggestions from the outside circle. (If the responses are outlandish or not in keeping with the situation as set forth, then this too is a proper subject for post-role-play discussion.)

It is very important that both during and after the role play, the role players not be criticized for their "acting." There is *no* wrong way to play a role. And in regard to acting ability, it should be emphasized that role playing has nothing to do with a theater production: the players are not performing for the amusement of their audience, but are generating specific data for later discussion and evaluation.

7.   In conducting the post-role-play discussion, perhaps the most important factor for the teacher to remember is that, of the myriad of useful data generated by a role play, students may see some things as important which the teacher may not have intended to focus on. So the teacher will have to judge just how far he is willing to stray from his particular objectives in following the interests of the students.

My strong preference is to open the floor to discussion with a nondirective statement like "Comments?" and let the discussion follow from there. I have found that my main objectives have almost always been touched upon by student-initiated discussion, and that these free discussions generally produce cogent points which I might have overlooked. If, on the other hand, an important area seems to have been neglected, the teacher can initiate an investigation of that area with a probe like one of the following:

"How did it feel to be a Dad in that situation?"

"What might be the consequences of doing that?"

"Let's see if we can generate some alternatives."

"What sort of relationship do you see here?"

"How well do they seem to be communicating their concerns to each other?"

"From what you have seen, what do you think are Sue's main objectives at this point?"

In this kind of probing, it is important to avoid the appearance of fishing for the one right answer. Students delight in playing "Guess What the Teacher's Thinking Of," and teachers often get sucked into delivering lectures via a series of leading questions. But such an approach tends to diminish the natural inquisitiveness of the students, while reinforcing the notion that the teacher is the fount of all wisdom.

Beware, too, the appearance of having in mind a predetermined outcome for the role play. If the students believe that the teacher is secretly trying to have them decide that Sue should not go to the concert, then the role play will be less spontaneous —perhaps a hypocritical performance for the teacher's benefit, or a defiant "acting out" of their resentment at being manipulated. In either case, the focus on genuine inquiry will be lost.

During this post-role-play discussion, it may be appropriate to resume role playing. The class can continue from the point at which the original role play had been cut off; or go back to the beginning, before Sue and Dad had said a word; or move far ahead in time (as, for instance, moving ahead to the meeting between Sue and Jim just before the concert). The purpose of resuming role-play activity can be to test an alternative response or action, to check out the probable consequences of a decision, or simply to generate more data for discussion. Depending on the situation, a new set of players can be recruited, or the original ones can continue. As with the original role play, the time limit should be announced at the outset.

A special note of advice is in order for the post-role-play discussion: The teacher should be particularly aware of the needs and feelings of the students who took part in the role play. The experience of role playing sometimes evokes strong or unusual emotions from those who participated, and these can best be dealt with by allowing the participants to talk openly about the experience for as long as they feel the need to talk. In directing the discussion, the teacher should generally give precedence to participants over observers, following their line of discussion for as long as seems appropriate. Furthermore, it is wise to plan to have ample time (at least twenty minutes) before the end of the period for the post-role-play discussion to take place.

Variations and Extensions

Once the class has learned the basic format for the *Decisions Open-Chair Role Play*, then three elaborations can be introduced: the temporary-member place, the alter-ego voice, and role-reversal.

The temporary-member place offers the students on the outside circle an opportunity to contribute to the role play in the following way:

A place on the floor next to each of the open chairs is designated as the temporary-member place. Any student on the outside circle may come into the role play as a third player by sitting in the temporary-member place. He may remain in the role play for two exchanges, after which he must move back into the outer circle.

The alter-ego voice speaks the messages which may be hidden under the surface dialogue. For instance, when Dad asks Sue, "How old are you?" his hidden message may be, "I'm trying to find an excuse not to let you go," or "I don't trust you." When any member of the outer circle identifies what he thinks is a hidden message, he may raise his hand and speak that message. Or, more dramatically, he may get up and stand or kneel behind the person who has spoken the surface message, and then deliver the real message.

The players may respond to the surface message or to the hidden message, as they choose (just as in the real world, persons sometimes respond directly to a hidden message—"You seem to be saying that you don't trust me"). It should be emphasized that a player who has sent a hidden message has not made a "mistake" or done something "wrong." The purpose of the alter-ego voice is not to show up the mistakes of the players, but to help students become more aware of the different levels of meaning that are constantly present in interpersonal communication.

It is also important to realize that there is no right or wrong in the hidden message as reported by an alter-ego voice. If an alter-ego voice hears a message that no one else hears, this just demonstrates the complex of meanings that may be present in any message.

NOTE: One way to start identifying hidden messages is to listen carefully to questions. Questions almost always contain an underlying statement. And as Fritz Perls points out in *Gestalt Therapy Verbatim,* statements almost always have hidden commands under them. For instance:

How are you?	Let's have a conversation.
When did you get home last night?	I'm worried that you might have been doing something that I disapprove of.
It's a beautiful day.	I want you to agree with me.
That's a pretty dress.	I want you to appreciate yourself.

Role-reversal is a useful technique, especially when one or both sides have become locked into positions of intransigence: Cut the role play, ask the players to move to the opposite position and to take up the role of the other character. Thus the Sues become Dads and move to Dad's side, the Dads become Sues and move to Sue's side. Then the role play can be continued from the point of interruption, or the enactment can be started again from the beginning. This technique can be a powerful way to highlight the underlying themes of an argument. Role-reversal helps students to develop their powers of empathy because it fosters emotional understanding as well as intellectual recognition of an alien point of view.

The Decisions Open-Chair format has been used successfully with students in junior high school through college. The open chair and the brainstorming of decision areas lowers the level of risk and allows students to bring their real concerns into the classroom with a degree of anonymity. After all, the situation that is the focus of the role play doesn't belong to a particular student in the class: it's a made-up situation involving a fictitious person, and the students who play the parts are playing not themselves but fictitious persons. In other words, the students can work on concerns which are relevant to their present lives without having to "own" the problem under discussion.

Furthermore, because several students play each part, the focus is not so much on the students-as-players as it is on the situation. And finally, because the material is generated from the class itself and because the situation is spontaneous and unfolding, the role play is potentially intriguing for the observers as well as for the participants.

While this role-playing format was developed specifically to identify and explore student concerns, it has been used with good success to examine specific works of literature, and to explore specific periods in history as well. For instance, in studying

Marjorie Kinnan Rawlings' *The Yearling*, one possible situation for role playing occurs when Jody is about to tell his mother that Flag, his pet fawn, has just destroyed the family's winter supply of corn. One open chair would represent Jody; the other one, his mother. Or in studying the Civil War, a Northern Congressman and a Southern Congressman could be debating the abolition of slavery.

A less obvious, but very meaningful, use of role play to enhance concepts studied in history or literature would be for the teacher to set up parallel situations which raise similar issues but relate directly to the students' lives. For *The Yearling*, the situation could be that Bill is about to tell Mother that while he and a friend were playing catch, his friend accidentally threw the ball through the kitchen window. For the study of issues in the Civil War, the situation could be that a Southern tobacco planter and a Northern legislator debate a law that will make cigarettes illegal because they have been found to be hazardous to health.

While these parallel situations may not deal with all of the "academic" issues under study, role play does free students from the need to follow a "script" to make the situation come out the way it did in the original story or in history. Role playing should thus be differentiated from "acting out" the scene. In "acting out," the actors perform what is more or less a set part, to dramatize for the audience what happened. In role playing, the players develop the situation spontaneously so that they and the on-lookers will have experiential material to examine. Of course, the acting out of predetermined situations is as legitimate a teaching technique as is role playing. The choice of technique would be determined by the teacher's objectives.

Pointers for Leading Decisions Role Play

Here's a brief synopsis of the key elements to keep in mind when leading a Decision Role Play:

1. Avoid overdeveloping the background to the situation. Instead, allow the players to develop their own background material as they need it. This helps keep the focus on the here and now.

2. Don't worry about inconsistencies between different players portraying the same character or between the unfolding action and the initial situation. These will work themselves out, and the inconsistencies can provide valuable discussion material.

3. Nothing is irrelevant. All behaviors, even total avoidance of the issue, provide useful and productive material for exploration.

4. Cut the role play at or before the given time limit. Never let it drag out.

5. In post-role-play discussion, use probes to explore issues:

    a. Ask for predictions as to the final outcome of the situation on the basis of the action so far.

    b. Brainstorm possible alternatives.

    c. Brainstorm possible consequences.

    d. Ask for opinions about the kind of relationship that has been portrayed.

    e. Ask for comments on the nature of the communication between the characters, and on the hidden agendas of the characters.

    f. Ask for ways that the conflict might be reduced so that the characters can work for a no-lose outcome.

Format for Confrontation Situation

The teacher may find that the format below will help in setting up a particular role play:

Issue: _____

Characters confronting the issue: (List only two and state their relationship.)

_____

_____

Situation: (What is one character asking or telling the other regarding some *action to be taken* which relates to the issue?)

_____

_____

_____

Time and place (if these are important considerations):

_____

_____

Students generally seem more interested in role-playing situations which they have developed themselves. A certain sense of commitment develops, and they find the material more relevant to their own lives.

The following procedure can be used by the teacher to guide students in developing their own situations: Divide the class into groups of four or five and ask each group to brainstorm for four minutes on issues which the class might consider. Next, give each group a five-minute period to select one issue and develop a situation from the issue, using the format provided above. Each situation is then read to the whole class, and the class votes by secret ballot on the first situation to be enacted. (The secret ballot allows students to explore issues which they might be reticent to express interest in publicly.)

Here are some confrontation situations developed by students for Decisions Role Play:

Issue: Peer pressure.

Characters: Jim, a boy of thirteen who wants to be a member of the in-group, and Joe, leader of the in-group.

Situation: Jim wants to join the group. Joe tells him the initiation feat is to break the antenna off the principal's car.

Time and Place: Playground at recess.

Issue: Personal independence vs. responsibility to parents.

Characters: Ann, a sophomore in college, and Ann's mother.

Situation: Ann is about to tell her mother that she is planning to spend Thanksgiving vacation alone with Tom, a senior at the same college.

Time and Place: The kitchen, early November.

Issue: Drugs.

Characters: Fred, a fifteen-year-old boy, non-user but curious, and Bill, leader of the local pill poppers.

Situation: Bill has a new pill that's "really mellow." He invites Fred to the Saturday party.

Time and Place: The school corridor on Thursday.

Issue: Sex.

Characters: Jane, a ninth-grader, and Sam, her regular boy friend, a tenth-grader.

Situation: All of Sam's friends are "doing it" and Sam is interested in "deepening his relationship" with Jane. Both are virgins.

Time and Place: Recess at school.

Issue: Sex.

Characters: Carol, an eleventh-grader, and Carol's regular boy friend, Ed, also in the eleventh grade.

Situation: All of Carol's girl friends are sleeping with their boys, and she thinks she's missing something. Ed is worried that it will "cheapen" their relationship. Both are virgins.

Time and Place: Walking home after school.

Issue: Pregnancy.

Characters: Helen and Mary, two sixteen-year-olds.

Situation: Helen thinks that she is pregnant. She is about to ask Mary, her "more experienced" friend, for advice.

Time and Place: During school, in the girls' locker room.

Issue: College career.

Characters: Betty, a college sophomore, and Dr. Frank, Betty's advisor.

Situation: Betty would like to drop out of college for a year to "find herself." She has no real plans except to get a job waitressing somewhere so that she can be independent. She needs Dr. Frank's approval if she is to be allowed to return to college in good standing.

Time and Place: Dr. Frank's office, mid-November of Betty's sophomore year.

Issue: Dropping out of high school.

Characters: Peter, a high school junior with a C+ average, and Peter's father.

Situation: Peter, who has just turned sixteen, has decided to drop out of school; he feels bored. He plans to get a job pumping gas. He is about to tell his father.

Time and Place: Dad's study, February of Peter's junior year.

Issue: Sex roles.

Characters: Bill and Mary, a married couple in their early thirties, parents of three children.

Situation: The couple has decided that three children are enough. Mary suggests a vasectomy for Bill. Bill suggests tubal ligation for Mary.

Time and Place: The living room after the children are in bed.

Footnotes

1.   What follows is based on an actual session conducted by the author with twenty-five tenth-grade students.

2.   Use a name that is not represented in the class.

3.   If the floor is not carpeted, throw rugs or pillows may be used, or simply paper mats. Having the players sit on the floor creates the feeling of an amphitheater, improves the sight lines of the outer circle, and emphasizes the significance of the open chairs.

Chapter Two

FORMATS

The Decisions Open-Chair Role Play described in the previous chapter is but one of an almost endless variety of formats for role playing. This chapter is intended to provide a kind of overview of the various forms. Certainly, no teacher will want to use every form; a variety of forms is presented so that individual teachers may choose the ones that seem most appropriate to their teaching styles and to the particular needs of their classes.

Levels of risk and personal involvement vary widely from one format to another. This is an important factor to consider in opting for a particular form of role play. Some teachers feel strongly that the school should not deal with the students' personal problems, while others feel equally strongly that helping the young cope with maturation is the central role of the school. Whatever a teacher's view may be, role playing is a vital teaching technique because it can be used to explore both personal concerns and academic subject matter. Teachers should identify their objectives, and choose the format(s) which they feel will work best.

Blackboard Role Play

This is a low-risk form of role play which can quickly generate a large body of data for discussion.

The teacher draws a circle face on the blackboard, and gives the class a little information about the character. He asks the class to think how this character would feel in a given situation. Students should think out loud, talking as the character might or responding to the character.

For example, let's say that the teacher wants to get at the problem facing a new student who comes into a home room which is fairly cohesive, and whose members tend to exclude newcomers. The teacher might use the circle face to represent a boy or girl who has just come to a class—or club or other group—where it seems that most of the other people already know each other. The class is asked to think of when they might have found themselves in this situation. (The teacher might prime the pump with one or two of his own personal experiences.)

After several students have given examples from their own experience, the teacher asks the class to imagine someone else in such a circumstance, and to say some of the thoughts that might be going on inside that young person's head. These thoughts can be voiced at random by any of the students, and there need not be any coherence or logical relationship between the thoughts expressed. The rules of brainstorming (see page 26) should apply here, especially the rule against negative evaluation.

After random thoughts have been expressed, at least two options are open: The class can discuss the problems of the newcomer, and determine what the newcomer—and the other members of the group or class—can do to help ease the tension. Or, the teacher can draw a second face on the board to represent one of the members of the in-group, and ask the class to say what thoughts this person might have when he sees a newcomer enter the group. Members of the class can "think out loud" for the in-group member.

As a further step, these two sets of concerns— the new member's and the old member's—can be compared and analyzed. Then, if the teacher wishes to continue exploring the topic through role playing, he can propose a conversation between the two circle faces, in which any volunteer may take part.

If it seems appropriate, the teacher might ask the students to brainstorm ways of handling this situation—what the newcomer might do to gain acceptance quickly, and how a member of the in-group might accommodate the new member without violating any pre-established prerogatives.

If this topic is used in a class which includes

only one newcomer, the exercise may seem to be directed at that individual. But the teacher can point out that the discussion is not merely for the newcomer's benefit, but for the personal growth of every student. We all encounter situations in which we are the outsider facing an established group. And in today's highly mobile society, in which the average family moves every five years, the ability to initiate and maintain membership in a group is an important skill for all. The problem is a very real one for many high school seniors who face the prospect that the group they've been with for so long is breaking up and scattering to different colleges and jobs.

Blackboard role plays can be developed to explore many different situations, and are appropriate to use at all levels from early elementary through high school and college.

Here are some examples of other situations which can be explored through blackboard role playing:

SHARING THE PLAYGROUND EQUIPMENT: the child who never gets a chance at the swings and the child who hogs the swings.

CHOOSING UP SIDES: the "captain" of the team and the child who is always picked last.

"BORROWING" BOOKS, CLOTHING, BASEBALL GLOVES, ETC. WITHOUT PERMISSION FROM THE OWNER: the "borrower" and the one "borrowed from."

CLEANING UP THE MESSY HOMEROOM: the messers and the janitor.

RIPPING OFF A CANDY STORE: the person stealing the candy bar and the manager of the store.

DRUGS: a person being offered a pill for the first time and the one offering the pill.

PREGNANCY: a fifteen-year-old girl who has just missed her period and the boy whom she thinks is responsible.

PARENTAL AUTHORITY AND CONTROL: the parent of a young person who has just stayed out all night and the young person.

For the situations above, one role can be played at a time or both faces can be put on the board so that a dialogue can occur.

In exploring situations such as the ones above, I have found that it is best not to try to maneuver the students into reciting pious truths such as "it's wrong to steal," or "we should all share." The value of these role plays is to expand the students' awareness of other points of view which can later be integrated into their decision-making processes.

Blackboard Press Conference

The Blackboard Press Conference format is similar to the Blackboard Role Play except that here the emphasis is impersonal—generating questions and possible answers about an author, a character from literature, a historical figure, or a person in current events.

The teacher draws the circle face and introduces the character to the class:

"This is Hamlet. You've read the play; now what questions do you have for the main character?"

Then students suggest questions to ask the character and the teacher lists the questions on the board. After five or six questions have been generated, the teacher asks if anyone would care to volunteer to speak for Hamlet and answer any of the questions that have been raised. More than one person can supply an answer to a question, and it doesn't matter if answers are contradictory.

The teacher's job is not to arbitrate between right and wrong answers, but to create an atmosphere in which all views can be aired freely. For instance, if the question is, "Why didn't you kill Claudius while he was praying?" one student might answer, "I was afraid that his soul would go to heaven if I killed him at such a moment." Another might say, "I was about to, but then I began to worry that my eyes and ears were deceiving me and he wasn't really guilty after all." Here the teacher could say, "Okay, any other answers for Hamlet? Or any comment on these answers?"

As in brainstorming, the teacher refrains from evaluative comment so that he will not suppress the students' desire to volunteer. If a student says something that is clearly in factual error, even this should be permitted to stand for the moment; chances are that another student will pick up the error and an investigation of the facts will follow naturally. If this does not occur, the teacher can come back to the point later and ask for clarification or confirmation from the text.

Not only does the press conference provide an intriguing springboard to discussion, but it is also a useful diagnostic and evaluative tool for the teacher. The Blackboard Press Conference points up the interests and concerns of students, and diagnoses their level of information.

Here are some other themes for the Blackboard Press Conference:

President Lincoln is being interviewed

after signing the Emancipation Proclamation.

Robert Frost is interviewed by a group who have just read "The Road Not Taken."

President Ford is interviewed on the subject of inflation.

A college admissions officer is interviewed on the topic, "What We're Looking for at X College."

A doctor is interviewed on why he chose the medical profession, or his particular area of specialization.

In addition, some intriguing blackboard press conferences can be held with objects—a talking nuclear power plant, a human heart, a seed, a new automobile, etc.

Open-Chair Press Conference

This format is similar to the Blackboard Press Conference, except that here the person to be interviewed is represented by an open chair with a paper face taped to the back. A panel of three or four students sits at the front of the room to speak for the open chair. Members of the class ask any questions they think of. Any of the students who are speaking for the open chair may answer.

This is an especially useful form of role play when a small group has prepared a special project for presentation to the rest of the class. For example, if the area of study is modern poetry, the students can be divided into small groups, each group responsible for preparing a class on one poet from a given list. The group may assign the entire class a few poems from the work of their poet beforehand, so that the interviewers will be able to ask informed questions. Then, on "W. H. Auden Day," for instance, the group role plays Auden by giving a reading from his works, or expounding his literary theories. This presentation is followed by a press conference about Auden's life and work.

This technique is well adapted to topics from the history curriculum. Each small group can study a separate topic in a broad given area, such as major battles of the Civil War. The group's report is given in the form of a press conference conducted by one of the principals, perhaps a general, involved in the battle.

For career education, each group can be responsible for finding out as much as possible about a given occupation (the list having been previously determined by the class). The group gives its report in a press conference, perhaps making a brief prepared statement first and then opening the floor to questions.

For science, a press conference may be held in which a noted research scientist is interviewed; the object of investigation itself may be interviewed. ("I'm an internal combustion engine—what would you like to know about me?")

NOTE: During any press-conference role play, there may be questions which the role players cannot answer—either because of lack of information or because the question calls for some value judgment which is beyond the scope of the role player. When such a situation occurs, it should not be considered as displaying the students' lack of preparation, but rather should be treated as an opportunity for further investigation of content or for an exploration of values.

If a student has missed or forgotten some obvious piece of information, such as the age of the poet, he himself will be very much aware that he was not as informed as he should have been, and he and his group will be better prepared in the future. Other groups will also learn from this experience to pay closer attention to pieces of information they ought to have command of. In order to preserve the enthusiasm and willingness of the students, the teacher should resist the temptation to criticize a poor job of preparation—it will be perfectly obvious anyway—and should discourage put-downs by members of the class ["Aw, he never does anything right!"].

Individual Press-Conference Role Play

The Blackboard Press Conference and the Open Chair Press Conference are useful in providing an exercise with a low level of risk and plenty of group support. But when a student is willing and able, he should be allowed to play the role as an individual and field questions from other members of the class.

It is my strong belief, however, that this should be done only when a student volunteers without pressure, and when the student has full knowledge of the press-conference format beforehand.

To build up confidence gradually, the Individual Press Conference can be used in conjunction with the Open-Chair Press Conference. After having the experience of playing a role as part of a group, some members of the class may be willing to take on that role as individuals. While the teacher should encourage this initiative, he must be very careful not to devalue the efforts of those who prefer to use the open chair and remain part of a group. If the students sense that the teacher has a hidden agenda in which, ideally, all of his students take on the role play as individuals, then the pressure to conform to (or rebel against) the teacher's expectations will increase. The risk of failure will become greater, which in turn may raise the level of anxiety and thus increase the actual chances of failure.

Historical and Literary Impersonations

Historical and literary impersonations differ from the individual press conference in that they are more in the nature of a prepared dramatic presentation, complete with costumes and rehearsed parts.

Historical impersonations have been used with great success in some fifth grade classes in the Fairfax, Virginia, public schools. Each student selected a historical figure from the period under investigation, researched information about his or her choice, and then prepared a short "autobiographical" presentation. Costumes were used to add to the effect. The presentations were so successful that they were repeated at a parent assembly and later before classes of third graders from the same school.

As an elaboration of this technique for older students, small groups of two, three, or four can combine to present a dramatic interlude or a "debate"—as, for instance, between Thomas Jefferson and Alexander Hamilton on the shape that the new government should take.

Literary impersonations can be used as an alternative to traditional book reports. Each student prepares a dramatic presentation in the role of the author or a main character from his or her book.

Incidental Role Plays

Once the class has been introduced to role playing through a session such as open-chair or blackboard role playing, there may be occasions when the teacher may wish to use an impromptu role play to clarify a question or illustrate a point.

For instance, let's say that the class has been discussing the difficulties involved in communicating with parents. The situation revolved around getting permission to stay out late on Saturday night. One student asks, "What should I do when my mother starts bringing up other things and doesn't answer my question?" The teacher says, "Okay, go ahead. You be your mother, and I'll be you. Show us what you mean."

During the role playing that follows, the teacher might wish to expand participation by saying, "Anyone want to help Billy speak for his mother?" or, "I need some help. How would some of you answer if you were Billy?"

Generally, these impromptu role plays should be brief and informal. The purpose is not necessarily to solve problems within the role play, but rather to make the situation concrete so that the discussion which follows will be more specific and direct.

Incidental role playing is also a useful counseling device, especially when role-reversal is employed to help an individual see another person's point of view. Suppose a high school student comes to his advisor and says, "I'm having a problem deciding what to do. I want to take the general course, but my father wants me to go to college, and he gets so mad that I can't even talk to him about it." The advisor could say, "Well, let's explore some of the reasons that your father feels that way. You be your father and start off by saying, 'I want my son to. . . .'" Here there is only one role, and the advisor acts as a listener and prompter, occasionally suggesting ideas for the role player to use. After two or three minutes of role playing, the advisor might break in and turn the focus to defining and solving the problem.

Occasions may arise in literature or history class which lend themselves to this kind of informal role playing. Suppose that the class is studying *Johnny Tremain,* and one of the students says, "I still don't see why Johnny was so mad at Dove." The teacher might say, "All right, this is a good point to explore. This half of the class be Johnny [pointing]. This half be Dove. The time is just after Johnny has burned his hand. Go ahead."

If the class is studying the history of the West, and a student asks, "Why were the ranchers against the farmers, anyway?" the teacher might ask the class to role play the two sides as above.

Once the students become accustomed to incidental role playing, the class can begin to snap in and out of role plays almost automatically when the occasion arises.

Six Characters in Search of a Novel[1]

It is my experience that role plays usually work best when there are only two roles—the focus is sharper, the lines of interaction are more clearly drawn. The form called Six Characters in Search of a Novel is an exception. This is a useful role play for exploring a work of literature or a historical event in which several important characters interact. (The role play can be further expanded by including the author as one of the principals.)

To begin the role play, the class sits in a circle and chooses parts. One quick way to do this is for the teacher to prepare large name tags bearing the characters' names, and then pass them out randomly. Depending on the number of students and the number of characters, two or three or even four students can be assigned the same character. All students playing the same role sit together. The teacher may allow a short period for each group to get together and discuss their character's particular perspective on the events under discussion, and to brainstorm a list of concerns that the character might have. Then the teacher throws the floor open to questions or comments. Any character can question or make a comment to any other character.

The task here is not an "acting" one: there is no need for the Hamlets to try to speak Elizabethan English. Rather, this is an opportunity to change from indirect questioning—*Why do you think Hamlet did that?*—to direct questioning—*Hamlet, why did you kill Polonius?*—and thus to bring a sense of immediacy to the discussion.

This kind of role play can continue for as long as the teacher feels it to be productive, or the teacher can break in at the end of a predetermined time to call for a discussion of the issues that have been raised. In either case, it is appropriate for the teacher to participate or cut into the role play for clarification or comment.

In addition, the alter-ego voice can be used where it seems useful: One member of each team is designated to be the alter-ego voice for that team. This person is empowered to ask those embarrassing questions that the character himself would hesitate to ask, and he can interpret any message that his character sends or receives in terms of its hidden content.

In cases where the students need help in learning what type of questioning is most productive, the teacher can provide model question stems such as the following:

[_____], how did you feel when I . . . ?

[_____], how could I have helped you when . . . ?

[_____], how could you have helped me when . . . ?

[_____], what objective did you have in mind when you . . . ?

[_____], if you had known that . . . , what would you have done?

[_____], how did you feel when . . . ?

[_____], what did you think when . . . ?

If the role plays seems to be dominated by one or two of the students representing the main characters, the teacher can call for brief rounds of questioning in which each character gets a chance to ask a question in turn or, conversely, in which each character is the focus of the questioning.

In social studies, the possibilities of this format are virtually limitless, for topics relating to both historical and current situations. International crises and conferences offer particularly fertile areas in which to role play public negotiations and/or the behind-the-scenes discussions and bargaining that take place between the parties beforehand. Some possibilities from recent history are the Potsdam Conference, any of the major questions which the U.N. has faced, and critical meetings of regional international organizations such as the O.A.S. or N.A.T.O., meetings between Kissinger and Mao, between Nixon and Brezhnev, between Solzhenitsyn and the Western press.

The American political process affords numerous opportunities for this kind of role play: the negotiations, both on and off stage, which led to the signing of the Declaration of Independence, the progress of the Missouri Compromise through Congress, the struggle in Congress over the dismantling of the Office of Economic Opportunity—all these are examples of situations in which students assume roles of historical persons with verifiable attitudes. Presidential or local election campaigns offer both historical and topical roles.

For current events, the role play can involve a discussion of a specific event or proposal, or of the general principle involved, with the discussants assigned roles as members of various interest groups. For example, in discussing a proposed program of federally subsidized medical care, the roles might include a black mother from an urban ghetto, the president of the American Medical Association, a young intern, a suburban middle-class housewife, the president of a large oil company, etc.

For these uses, it will most likely be appropriate for the members of each role team to meet briefly to discuss their position. It is important to try to steer the role play clear of stereotyping, especially in cases such as the current events issue above.

Another possibility is to have the role teams retain their roles over a more extended period of time. This allows for a deeper exploration of the issue from a particular point of view and, in historical cases, allows time for verification of the role assumptions if desired.

Conflicts Role Play[2]

This role play has been used with much success in human relations programs for both college and upper-level high school students. Students find this form of role playing particularly compelling because it deals with the real concerns of the members of the class.

The teacher passes out four-by-six index cards and asks the students to describe briefly—and anonymously—a conflict they are having with some other person. If the student cannot think of a current conflict, he may make one up, or he may describe a conflict that he has had, or a situation that he is familiar with but not directly involved in. Also, he may turn in a blank card if he wishes. The cards are returned to the teacher face down, and shuffled. A card is drawn at random as the first situation to role play.

Here are some examples of conflicts which have been successfully role played:

RELIGION: Mother wants her daughter to attend church, but the daughter feels that there are other appropriate ways of worship.

PERSONAL APPEARANCE: Father thinks his son's long hair is effeminate.

USE OF FAMILY CAR: Daughter is required to drive her younger siblings to lessons, appointments, etc., but is denied the use of the family car for an evening date.

HOME TIES: Mother is upset because her daughter at college neglects to write her at least weekly.

ROOMMATE CONFLICTS: One roommate continually keeps late hours, entertaining friends in the room, while the other would like to study or sleep.

DATING PROBLEMS: He claims that she

doesn't really love him because she won't go to bed with him.

MONEY: Mother insists on accompanying her son to buy clothing, since once he came home with a motorcycle jacket which she didn't like.

PERSONAL PRIVACY: Daughter discovers that her mother has been secretly reading her letters.

HOUSEHOLD RESPONSIBILITIES: Son has been assigned to wash dishes every night and mow the lawn on weekends but feels that this is being done to keep him from associating with friends, whom his parents disapprove of.

SIBLING CONFLICTS: Girl borrows her older sister's cardigan sweater without permission and then stains it.

For the role play itself, the open-chair format can be used (as in the Decisions Open-Chair Role Play described in Chapter One), or individual students can assume each of the roles, depending upon the level of risk and the availability of volunteers. Another possibility is to divide the class into groups, with each group playing one of the roles. In any case, the role play should be timed, and the teacher should assure the players that he will cut the role play at the precise end of the stated period of time (four or five minutes is usually sufficient). The role play should be followed by a discussion of the issues that have been raised, with the emphasis on ways of resolving the conflict. Suggested resolutions can be role played where this seems appropriate.

In directing the post-role play discussion, the teacher might focus on the following sequence:

1. Determine the source of the conflict. What conflicting desires underlie the situation?

2. Generate several alternative courses of action which the person could use to reduce the conflict. What are some of the other paths which have not been explored through the role play?

3. Explore the risks involved in following some of those alternatives. How would the other person be likely to react? Would this course of action reduce the conflict or increase it?

4. Consider whether there needs to be some preliminary groundwork in opening communication before this subject is raised. What areas of agreement and support can be established?

5. How can the subject be approached so that the focus is on the problem rather than on the personalities? How can the issue be raised in a way

which does not threaten the other person and thereby close off communication?

During and after the role play, the teacher should be careful to preserve the anonymity of the situation. In their enthusiasm, students sometimes will start to guess whose conflict has been presented or may interrupt the role play with a comment like, "I think I know whose situation this is and that's not really the way it happened." The teacher might respond in the following way: "We have collected these situations under the rules of strict confidence and anonymity, and I feel that it is most important to preserve that trust and confidence. Please refrain from acting in a manner which may give clues as to the author of a given situation." On the other hand, if the individual wishes to reveal himself, there is no reason why he should not do so, as long as this doesn't become established as a norm and thus force others to do the same.

Secrets

This is a powerful role-playing activity to be used only where a high level of trust and intimacy has developed in the class. Each student writes down a personal secret on a four-by-six card. (The secret can be real or invented.) Next, the cards are collected and shuffled and placed in a stack at the front of the room. Each student comes forward in turn, picks a card from the pile, reads it aloud, and then continues to talk as though the secret were his or her own. (If the student selects his own secret, he may replace it and draw another, or he may read and play the secret in the usual way.) After each brief role play, the class can discuss the secret and brainstorm possible solutions if the secret involves a problem to be overcome.

This sharing of secrets generally has a powerful community-building effect on the group as they recognize and affirm the commonalities which run through their individual hopes and fears. Occasionally, there is a sentiment expressed at the end of this activity that everyone should identify his or her own secret. It is my feeling that the teacher should resist this and uphold the right of even a small minority who might not wish to reveal themselves as the authors of particular secrets. Retroactive changing of the rules such as this may also lead some students to be less candid in later activities.

Possessions

This activity is similar to "Secrets," except that the content is less emotionally charged. Each student (and the teacher, too, if he or she wishes) writes a short paragraph describing a prized possession. The paragraphs are collected and placed in a stack at the front of the room. Each student comes forward in turn, draws a card, reads the description, and then continues to talk about the possession, explaining, perhaps, how he or she acquired the possession, what pleasant memories the possession brings, or what he or she may wish to do with the possession in the future.

This role play has been used by teachers of public speaking and oral composition as an intriguing topic for extemporaneous speaking. Other subjects which could be role played in this manner include "An embarrassing moment," "The high point of my vacation," "My favorite relative," "One moment when I was scared out of my wits," etc.

Possessions and similar role plays are useful for building empathy and a sense of community.

Problem Story Role Play[3]

For this type of role play, the teacher reads a brief story which develops a problem to be faced by the characters. The story ends without a solution, and the students are asked to role play possible outcomes. One book which is devoted almost entirely to the exposition of problem story role playing is *Role-Playing for Social Values* by Fannie R. Shaftel with stories by George Shaftel. Each problem story in the Shaftels' book is designed to teach a social value from among the following divisions:

1. Individual Integrity, including such issues as honesty, responsibility for others, fairness, and individual integrity versus group integrity.

2. Group Responsibility, including sections on accepting others and sensitivity training.

3. Self-Acceptance.

4. Managing One's Feelings.

The recent work of Lawrence Kohlberg (see Chapter Five, "Role Playing and the Development of Moral Judgment"), which stresses developmental stages in moral concepts, leads me to believe that the division of social values into such virtues as honesty, fairness, etc., for the purposes of teaching does not have a sound basis in psychological theory. Nonetheless, role playing of problem stories allows students to explore moral issues at their own developmental level. The teacher who uses these methods should be warned, however, not to expect quick, dramatic changes in attitudes or behavior from these techniques, which are essentially long-range in their effect.

An example of the problem story technique is

the Shaftels' story "Paper Drive," which is designed to explore issues of honesty and cheating. In this story the teacher of a sixth-grade class discovers that her students have won the community paper drive contest by concealing pieces of junk metal in their bundles of paper in order to increase the bundles' weight. When she confronts them with this fact, they claim that they were getting back at their rivals who were spraying their paper with water in order to make it heavier, and then covering the outside of the bundles with dry paper. Since the rival class came in second in the paper drive, if the teacher turns in her class for cheating, then the rival class may win through cheating. What is the teacher to do?

The Shaftels recommend several enactments followed by discussion. They suggest the following format:

1. A first enactment to define the specific events and to begin to analyze the problem.

2. A second and possibly a third enactment to explore the roles and feelings of those involved.

3. Later enactments to delineate events which lead to personal and social consequences.

4. Final enactments in which decisions are made.

5. Generalization through discussion, drawing

conclusions, and further applications of the principles involved.

The following problem story and ensuing role play is based on an actual experience with junior-high-school-aged boys:

"Trouble Money"

During the Youth Club's annual trip to Washington, D.C., Joe, Billy, and Fred, three fourteen-year-old club members, find a wallet on the grass near the swimming pool of the motel in which they are staying. The wallet contains forty dollars.

The boys take the wallet to their room to decide what to do. Although the owner's name and address are in the wallet, the three decide to split the money. Then there is the problem of what to do with the wallet, which still contains a driver's license, credit cards, and other identification. Unsure of what to do, the boys hide the wallet in one of their suitcases.

The next morning, the three boys slip away from the group and buy new clothes with the money. But that afternoon, Mr. Smith, the Club leader, calls the group together and says that he has heard that some of the members have found a wallet, and he feels that the group should consider what ought to be done in these circumstances.

Using the five steps recommended by the Shaftels, this problem story could be explored in the following way:

Step One: After the teacher has read the story to the class, three students are chosen to play the roles of Joe, Billy, and Fred for the first enactment. They start their scene at the moment that they discover the wallet. This enactment follows the events in the story, with the three boys finding the wallet, taking it to their room, deciding to split the money, and then hiding the wallet. (This first enactment is almost in the nature of a dramatic presentation in order to establish the specific events.)

Step Two: For the second enactment, three new players are chosen, and these three debate among themselves what they should do with the money and the wallet. Here the emphasis is on exploring the feelings and motives of those involved. For the third enactment, two players are chosen to play the two halves of Mr. Smith, the half which wants to get to the bottom of this matter, and the half which prefers to leave well enough alone and not get involved. Mr. Smith has overheard bits of conversation which lead him to believe that some of the members have found a wallet and taken the money. The two halves of Mr. Smith try to decide what to do.

Step Three: The three boys have spent the money. They discuss among themselves whether what they have done is right or not. Then the teacher asks them to reverse roles—to take on the role of the person who has lost the wallet and to discuss what he would like to have the finders do and why.

Step Four: The final enactment is the meeting of the entire group in which Mr. Smith explains the situation as he understands it and asks what should be done. One student plays the role of Mr. Smith, three students play Joe, Billy, and Fred, and the other members of the class play the other members of the group. The group tries to decide what should be done.

Step Five: After the final enactment, the entire class discusses the issues involved, drawing general principles and conclusions from this specific instance.

These enactments and discussions generally lead to socially acceptable conclusions—in this case, that the boys should have returned the money and wallet in the first place, and now they should find ways to earn the money and return it. However, the teacher should be under no illusions that the students will be able to generalize from the problem story situation and follow the principles involved in their own future actions. Rather than hoping for a specific change of behavior as the outcome, the teacher can define his objectives as raising issues of social and moral values for students to explore and deliberate. It is through this process of raising, discussing, and reflecting on problems involving social and moral consequences that young persons grow in their powers of moral reasoning. (See Chapter Six, "Role Playing and Moral Judgment.")

Teachers and students can make up their own problem stories, or they may use the forty-six problem stories in the Shaftels' book.

Parts-of-Self Role Play

This is an extension of either the Decisions or the Conflicts Role Play, for use where the decision to be made or the conflict to be resolved is internal to the character. For instance, Tom is deciding whether to go to college or enlist in the Army. One chair represents College Tom and the other chair, Army Tom. Teams can speak for each chair, as in the Decisions Role Play; or an individual can sit in each chair to take the role represented by that chair; or one individual can take on both roles, moving back and forth between the two chairs.

It is possible to divide the self into more than

two parts. If Tom has a third option, such as to take a job pumping gas, then this potential role can become a third chair in the role play.

I-It Role Play

In his book, *To a Dancing God,* Sam Keen points out that one of the concerns of modern man is the clarification of his place in the technological world, the relationship of I to It. The Decisions Open-Chair Role Play format can be used to clarify this issue. For instance, one chair can represent Bill and the other can be the second-hand car that he has just bought, or the television set that seems to dominate his spare time, or the marijuana that he is tempted to smoke. As in the Decisions Role Play, the situation should be defined so that a specific, clear conflict exists.

For example, in the role play between Bill and his television set, Bill could be arguing with his set as to whether he should be studying for his math test or watching his favorite science-fiction program, or whether he should spend Sunday afternoon watching the football game or go out and play tennis. The role play between Bill and his car might focus on the amount of time that Bill has to work each week just to support his car; the car might point out that it needs a valve job, a new muffler, etc., while Bill might state his feelings that the car already demands too much.

In these role plays, it's important to dissuade students from paying lip service to what they think the teacher's values may be. The more open and accepting the teacher can be, the more likely it is that the role play will retain freshness and spontaneity and not degenerate into a contrived theater piece.

Multiple Role Plays

Some teachers have had great success in dividing their classes into small groups and having each small group pursue the topic through its own role play independent of the other groups. This gives more students a chance to take part in the role playing at the same time, and often generates a wider variety of data than the single role play. Students should, of course, be familiar with the techniques of role playing before they break into small groups. Following are some examples of multiple role play:

Advice[4]

The topic in this case is what course of action to take when another person comes to you for personal advice. First, the teacher asks the students to think of a time when a friend has come to them to ask their advice on a personal matter, or when they have gone to a friend or counselor for advice on a personal matter. The teacher does not ask the students to share this information; they are just to think about it.

The teacher presents the problem:

Judy, a high school junior, has just confessed to Jim, a high school senior, that she thinks she is pregnant as a result of their affair. Jim is flustered. He thinks he loves Judy and he feels responsible for her, but at the same time, he feels that he's too young to be tied down. He decides to seek advice and chooses Mrs. Brown, the mother of Bill, who is one of his best friends. Jim has found a time in the afternoon when Mrs. Brown is alone in her kitchen and he probably won't be seen entering or leaving.

If you were Mrs. Brown, how would you advise Jim? What would be your concerns? How would you handle the problem of confidentiality (since you are good friends with both Jim's and Judy's parents)? What sort of information do you think might be helpful to Jim? How would you deal with your own values? Would you try to get Jim to accept a solution that you offer, or would you let him work out his own solution?

The teacher divides the class into groups of four and asks the small groups to brainstorm possible answers to these questions and to discuss the answers for five to ten minutes, trying to form some conclusions and work out some plan of advice as a group.

At the end of the discussion period, the teacher asks for two volunteers from the class as a whole, one to play Jim, the other to play Mrs. Brown, in a short demonstration role play for the entire class. The role play should last no more than five minutes, after which the teacher asks for comments. He should find out whether or not Jim and Mrs. Brown of the role play followed the course of action determined by the small groups of which they were a part.

Then the teacher asks the students to move back into their groups of four so that each group can prepare to role play the situation. One person becomes Mrs. Brown; another becomes Jim; the third is the group leader, who starts and stops the role play; and the fourth (and fifth if there is one) is the observer, whose job it is to observe the interactions and comment at the end of the role play. Where practical, the observer may use the *Role-Playing Observer Sheet* on page 85.

After the roles have been assigned in each group, but before the role play actually begins, all the Jims change groups, so that each Jim will confront a different Mrs. Brown from the one with whom he has been discussing the situation. This cross-fertilization provides a certain dramatic tension and newness to the situation.

When the new groups are arranged, the teacher signals the group leaders to begin the role plays, reminding them that there will be ten minutes for the session, and that the group leaders should allow the role play to continue for no more than five minutes so that the post-role-play discussion can be at least five minutes long. At the end of the ten minutes, the teacher can lead a general class discussion, focusing on a variety of alternatives and the effect of each as seen in the role plays.

College Interview

This form of multiple role playing can be useful in preparing students to face a college interview, a job interview, or any similar situation. The teacher presents them with the following problem:

The college that you would like to attend is faced with the problem of having only one place for every six applicants. For this reason, the admissions officers have been charged with determining which of the applicants show seriousness of purpose and are specially suited to attend this college. What sorts of questions do you suppose college admissions interviewers might ask you under these circumstances, and how might you best respond?

The teacher divides the class into groups of

five or six and asks the students to discuss this problem for five minutes, trying to reach some conclusions as to the best approach to take when being interviewed. Then the members of each group choose one person to play the interviewee, two persons to play college interviewers, one role-play leader, and one or two observers. Before the role play, each interviewee is sent to another group where he will be interviewed by two college interviewers who have not been part of his discussion group. Ten minutes are allowed for the role play and the following discussions. The role-play leader in each group should cut the role play at the end of five minutes to allow time for reports from the observers and discussion.

After the role play and discussion, the interviewee returns to his own group, and the roles are rotated so that the observers and leader are now role players, and the role players are observers and leaders. Then the new interviewee can be sent to a different group and the role play repeated. At the end of this round, each group can make a short report to the class about what happened in the successive role plays. Finally, the teacher can lead a general discussion of the entire situation.

Role-Playing Observer Sheet

The Role-Playing Observer Sheet presented below is designed to help the observer focus his attention toward certain aspects of the role play. The sheet can be reproduced and handed out to each student, or simply written on the board for all to see. The Role-Playing Observer Sheet is especially useful for multiple role plays where the post-role play discussion takes place in small groups without the teacher. It can also be used, of course, with any of the other role plays in this book.

Role-Playing Observer Sheet

1. Characterize the opening exchange (cheerful, genial, guarded, threatening, questioning, bored, etc.).

2. How well did the participants listen to each other? Try to give a specific example of good or poor listening.

3. Characterize the participants' nonverbal behavior toward each other.

4. Did you hear any hidden messages? If so, jot down one or two.

5. Were there any turning points in the discussion? If so, where?

6. Characterize the behavior of the participants toward each other along the following continuums. Mark the initials of each role player at the appropriate place on each continuum.

ATTEMPTING TO CON-TROL THE OTHER	WILLING TO COOPERATE
SHOWING LACK OF CONCERN FOR OTHER'S FEELINGS	SHOWING CONCERN —EMPATHIZING
SHOWING SUPERI-ORITY TOWARD THE OTHER	SHOWING EQUALITY TOWARD THE OTHER
CLOSED TO IDEAS OF OTHER	OPEN TO IDEAS

Rank Orders and Role Playing

Role playing can be used to test out and to bring a sense of immediacy to a rank-order problem, as the following example suggests:[5]

In an exploration of the changing role of women in society, participants were asked to rank the following three conditions in order of their importance to themselves personally:

 a. Family unity—harmony.
 b. Economic advancement.
 c. Personal satisfaction and
   self-actualization.

Next the class was divided into groups of four or five, and the groups were given five minutes to develop role-play situations which would test the rankings. These situations would derive from the following basic formula, delineated by the teacher:

"Your group is to role play a family which is about to decide whether or not one of the adults should accept a job offer which will necessitate moving the whole family to a new location. Decide which family member each of you will play, what the present family and job situation is, who has been offered the new job, and what the new job entails."

Situations that participants have developed for this activity include the following:

1. The wife has been offered the post of dean at a large Southern university. The husband is assistant professor at a small New England college. Their ten- and twelve-year-old children are very happy in their schools and have many friends.

2. The husband, plant manager of a small factory in a town in Vermont, has just been offered a significant promotion into the management of the

parent company, located in New York City. The wife is very active in their town's civic affairs and is president of the local League of Women Voters. The husband's parents, who are living with the family, have lived all their lives in this town.

3. The sixteen-year-old daughter is told she has a very good chance of making the Olympic swimming team if the family can move to California, where she can practice regularly under instruction from the coach who produced three champions in the last Olympics. The rest of the family is happy in their home in a Midwestern community where the father is an insurance broker, the mother is active in community affairs, and the fourteen-year-old son is a stand-out in the local Babe Ruth League.

After the details of the role-play situation have been developed, each group has five minutes to role play its situation, working for a decision, while the other groups observe. If no decision is reached in the five minutes, the teacher can ask the observers to predict the eventual decision on the basis of what has been developed thus far. Finally, the participants are asked to compare the way they played their roles with their ranking on the original rank-order problem: did the role playing change, clarify, or strengthen their original positions? What new insights or perspectives have they gained regarding the issue from this role play?

I Am the Jury: A Four-Part Role Play

This role play is designed to explore the process of group decision making, focusing particularly on the uses of information in reaching a decision. The class is divided into four sections. Each section will form a jury which will deliberate on one of the four cases presented below. Each jury should see only its own case sheet, and the four discussions should take place in separate rooms, if possible. At the end of the ten-minute decision period, all the juries are brought together to report on their cases and the sentences that they have imposed. The four cases are compared, and a general discussion can follow.

Since the crime in each case is the same, one of the important issues for the discussion is whether the sentences in each case should be the same, or whether the background or personality of the individual involved should be taken into account. In other words, which information is relevant for the decision at hand, and which information is irrelevant?

If any jury reaches its decision before the ten-minute period is over, the members may spend the remainder of their time in preparing a brief explaining and supporting their decision, or they may consider what other sentences they might impose if they were not limited to the seven choices.

For classes that are unfamiliar with group process activities, it may be helpful to assign one or two process observers to each jury, using the *Role-Playing Observer Sheet* (see page 85).

For small classes, this role play can involve only two juries and two cases: either Cases One and Two, or Cases Three and Four.

I Am the Jury—Case One

The defendant, Sam Jones, has been found guilty of selling one five-dollar bag of marijuana to an undercover agent. Your charge is to determine the sentence which should be imposed.

THE FACTS: Sam is seventeen. He had a poor high school record and dropped out when he turned seventeen. He has had three jobs during the past year—pumping gas, washing dishes, and delivering groceries, but he is now without a job. He lives with an aunt in the poorer section of town, but he spends much of his time with a street gang known as the "Tigers." He is suspected of having been involved in a theft ring, but no hard evidence has been presented on this point. (The jury has been instructed to disregard testimony about this.) You must choose one of the following options:

1. Six months probation.

2. Six months probation, $100 fine.

3. One year probation, $500 fine.

4. Three months in a correctional institution.

5. Six months in a correctional institution.

6. One year in a correctional institution, possibility of early release for good behavior.

7. Two years in a correctional institution, possibility of early release for good behavior.

I Am the Jury—Case Two

The defendant, Sam Jones, has been found guilty of selling one five-dollar bag of marijuana to an undercover agent. Your charge is to determine the sentence which should be imposed.

THE FACTS: Sam is seventeen. He is in his senior year of high school and has an excellent academic record. In addition, he is a member of the varsity soccer team and has been been elected to the Student Council. His father is a prominent doctor, and Sam plans to study medicine himself. He was recently nominated as a candidate for the Rotary Club's School Citizenship Award, but the winners have not yet been announced. You must choose one of the following options:

1. Six months probation.

2. Six months probation, $100 fine.

3. One year probation, $500 fine.

4. Three months in a correctional institution.

5. Six months in a correctional institution.

6. One year in a correctional institution, possibility of early release for good behavior.

7. Two years in a correctional institution, possibility of early release for good behavior.

I Am the Jury—Case Three

The defendant, Sue Jones, has been found guilty of selling one five-dollar bag of marijuana to an undercover agent. Your charge is to determine the sentence which should be imposed.

THE FACTS: Sue is seventeen. She had a poor high school record and dropped out when she turned sixteen. She has had three jobs during the past year—as a counter girl in a short-order restaurant, as a dishwasher, and as a helper in a laundry and dry cleaning operation, but is now without a job. She lives with an aunt in the poorer section of town, but she spends much of her time with a street gang known as the "Tigers." She is suspected of having been involved in a theft ring, but no hard evidence has been presented on this point. (The jury has been instructed to disregard testimony about this.) You must choose one of the following options:

1. Six months probation.

2. Six months probation, $100 fine.

3. One year probation, $500 fine.

4. Three months in a correctional institution.

5. Six months in a correctional institution.

6. One year in a correctional institution, possibility of early release for good behavior.

7. Two years in a correctional institution, possibility of early release for good behavior.

I Am the Jury—Case Four

The defendant, Sue Jones, has been found guilty of selling one five-dollar bag of marijuana to an undercover agent. Your charge is to determine the sentence which should be imposed.

THE FACTS: Sue is seventeen. She is in her senior year of high school and has an excellent academic record. In addition, she is a member of the varsity field hockey team and has been elected a member of the Student Council. Her father is a prominent doctor, and Sue plans to study to become a doctor herself. She was recently nominated as a candidate for the Rotary Club's School Citizenship Award, but the winners have not yet been announced. You must choose one of the following options:

1. Six months probation.

2. Six months probation, $100 fine.

3. One year probation, $500 fine.

4. Three months in a correctional institution.

5. Six months in a correctional institution.

6. One year in a correctional institution, possibility of early release for good behavior.

7. Two years in a correctional institution, possibility of early release for good behavior.

Decision-Agent Role Play[6]

This role play can be used for teaching formal decision-making theory and presenting a step-by-step process for considering and making decisions. The following sequence is followed:

1. Define and clarify the problem.

2. Identify alternative solutions.

3. Consider the risks involved in each alternative.

4. Determine the probable consequences resulting from pursuing each alternative.

5. Identify the most desirable outcome.

6. Make specific plans to attain this outcome.

The decision agent is a mythical professional, similar to a doctor or lawyer, but one who is especially trained in helping people make decisions. A dilemma is presented to the class, involving a decision to be faced by an individual. The decision agent's task is to guide the individual through the above steps in helping him to reach his decision.

For instance, a college basketball star is offered a contract to play professional basketball at the end of his junior year. The decision for him to face is whether to obtain his college degree first, or to sign immediately, thus postponing his graduation from college. One student plays the basketball star and another student plays the decision agent. (This can also be done as an open-chair role play.)

The star has just entered the decision agent's

office to ask for help. Members of the class who are not playing roles are given *Decision Agent Process Observer Sheets* to fill out (see below). At the end of five minutes, the teacher cuts the role play and asks for comments from the observers, focusing on the questions from the *Decision-Agent Process Observer Sheet*.

Decision-Agent Process Observer Sheet

DIRECTIONS: Watch the role play carefully and jot down any notes that will help you to remember specific events. Use the following list of questions where appropriate:

1. Does the problem seem to be well defined? How does the decision agent help in defining the problem?

2. Are alternative solutions considered? Jot down those that are mentioned.

3. Are the consequences of various alternative solutions considered? If so, list some.

4. Are the risks of each alternative considered?

5. Has the most desirable outcome been identified? What is it?

6. What plans are made for attainment of a desirable outcome?

7. At the end of the role play, turn this sheet over and jot down questions that you would have liked to have had answered if you had been the individual faced with this decision. What additional information would help in making the decision?

The newspaper is a good source of problem situations for this role play. Generally, the teacher should read the entire news story to the class. Short stories and novels are also full of difficult decisions which characters must face, and which can be used for this role play.

Nonverbal Role Plays

Nonverbal role plays can be used to make students more aware of body language and other nonverbal cues in communication. Following are some frequently used nonverbal role plays. Remember, do not judge acting ability or place special emphasis on it.

Adverbs

The class is divided into two teams. Each team compiles a list of adverbs for members of the other team to act out. The adverbs are written on slips of paper, then, as in charades, the teams take turns competing in acting out the adverbs in the following way:

Team A gives one of its slips of paper to a member of Team B (or to a group of two or three members of Team B). The recipient of the slip must act out the adverb written on his slip of paper while his teammates try to guess what adverb he is acting. No props or sounds are allowed. Then Team B gives a slip of paper to a member(s) of Team A. The process is repeated until everybody has had a chance to act out an adverb. This game can be scored by recording the length of time it takes each team to guess the adverb. Lowest aggregate score wins.

—ly

In this variation of Adverbs, one person is designated to be "it" and sent out of the room while the others select an adverb. Then the person returns to the room and gives directions to the others. Examples: "Mary, walk in the manner of the word." "John, shake hands with Bill in the manner of the word." "Everybody, dance in the manner of the word." Then "it" trys to guess the word. For larger groups, two or more persons can be "it" at a time.

What's going on here?

A list of ten situations is handed out to each member of the class. For example:

1. Your team just scored a touchdown.

2. You are on your way to the doctor's office for a shot.

3. You are very hungry.

4. You are alone in the house and you've just heard a strange noise.

5. Your brother has just broken your record player.

6. You wanted to watch television and your mother has sent you to your room to do homework.

7. You're on your way to a party.

8. You've been sent to the principal's office for being late to class.

9. Today's lunch: pizza and ice cream.

10. The school bus has just left without you.

Then an individual or a small group is given a slip containing *one* of the ten situations. The student(s) acts out the situation for ten seconds, and then the rest of the class guesses which situation he has played. This procedure is repeated for the other situations.

Knock, Knock

Each member of the class is given a list of ten persons who might be knocking on the door. Then the teacher gives a student a slip of paper with one of the identities on it. The student goes out and knocks on the door, and the other students try to guess which person from the list the student is playing. Suggestions:

1. An encyclopedia salesman.

2. A policeman about to make an arrest.

3. A policeman bringing home a lost child.

4. A neighbor asking for a cup of sugar.

5. A neighbor asking you to turn down your record player.

6. The kid next door wanting Johnny to come out and play.

7. The kid next door trick-or-treating on Halloween.

8. The paper boy collecting his weekly pay.

9. A husband who has accidentally been locked out of his house.

10. Someone collecting for the Red Cross.

As a variation, one individual could make up his own situation and then portray it in pantomime before the class, knocking at a door where the others could see him.

Each role play should be followed by a discussion centering on the nonverbal cues which led to the correct identification of the role. If appropriate, identify other cues which sent contradictory messages.

Written Role Plays

Almost any oral role play can also be written. For instance, in the situation between Sue and her father (see Chapter One), all the students could be asked to write three minutes of spontaneous dialogue between the two characters. Then the teacher might ask each student to read his last two exchanges to the class and compare the differences and similarities. Or the students could get together in groups of three or four and read their role plays to one another, and then each group could report its findings to the whole class.

History and English teachers sometimes use written role plays as a form of examination. For instance: Write an internal dialogue for General Robert E. Lee, one voice urging that he accept the command of the Union Army, the other that he accept command of the Confederate Army. Or write a dialogue between the Jody we see in the first chapter of *The Yearling* and the Jody we see in the last chapter of *The Yearling*, the subject being whether or not he should have a deer for a pet.

"I Am the Picture" Written Role Play

This role play has been used with upper elementary, junior high school, and high school students as a means of identifying student concerns and as a community-building activity, as well as a written composition exercise.

The teacher posts a picture containing one or two figures and involving a situation which is in some way ambiguous. (The picture may be taken from a newspaper or magazine, or it may be a drawing, painting, or photograph.) The students are asked to concentrate on the picture and try to understand what is going on, using clues such as clothing, expressions, body language, or surroundings. Then the teacher asks the students to imagine that they *are* one of the figures and to complete the following sentence stems which are written on the board:

1. I've just come from . . .
2. Now I'm thinking about . . .

3. One thing that I'm afraid of is . . .

4. What I'd like to do most now is . . .

5. One question I have is . . .

6. I'm happiest when . . .

7. I feel most important when . . .

8. I'm saddest when . . .

9. If I could have one wish, it would be...

10. Right now I'd like to . . .

11. I like to be called . . .

The sentences can then be shared in small groups of five or six students. As an alternative to the sentence stem completion, or in addition to it, the teacher can ask each student to write a short story from the point of view of the figure. The stories can then be shared or posted on the wall.

Role Plays from Personal-Growth Activities and Values-Clarification Strategies

Many personal-growth activities and values-clarification strategies (see Bibliography) can be adapted to role plays, especially for the study of literature or history. Here are some examples:

Hamlet's Twenty Loves

Role play Hamlet as his character is presented at the beginning of the drama. Write a list of twenty things you (as Hamlet) love to do.[7] Code the twenty items in the following way: Place an A next to any item that you usually do alone, an O next to any item that you usually do with others. Place an M beside an item that your mother, Queen Gertrude, would approve of your loving. Place an exclamation mark next to any item that requires physical action, and a dash next to any item that requires physical passivity.

Napoleon's Thought Card

Role play Napoleon on the eve of the battle of Waterloo and write a short thought card, that is, list a few of the things that are on your mind.[8]

Teacher's Priorities

Role play your teacher and rank these three situations from the most important to the least important:

   a. You are known for the fine academic achievement of your students. They always do well on the SAT's.

   b. One of your students, who is considered to be a rather slow learner, produces an exciting, original piece of work.

c. It is not unusual for students to come to you to discuss their personal problems and concerns.

After you have ranked these situations, try to persuade the other "teachers" that they should adopt your rankings.

Hemingway's Possessions
Role play Ernest Hemingway and make a list of your five most prized possessions. (Invent them, don't do research.) All "Hemingways" read their lists to the class. The discussion which follows should center on the role players' reasons for their choices and the perceptions underlying these reasons. (Try also T. S. Eliot's five favorite foods.)

Guerrilla Theater

One of the most intriguing formats for role playing is Guerrilla Theater, or Street Theater. In this form of role playing, the objective is to raise the level of consciousness of observers—perhaps even to the point where they will change their behavior. Football pep rallies, parades, and protest marches often incorporate elements of guerrilla theater. The mock search-and-destroy mission staged in front of the U.S. Capitol by the Vietnam Veterans Against the War was an excellent example of guerrilla theater used for political purposes. And Shakespeare uses a form of guerrilla theater in the play-within-a-play in *Hamlet*, where Hamlet's avowed purpose is "to catch the conscience of the King."

School assemblies make good settings for in-school guerrilla theater, staging anything from clowns running down the aisles advertising the Junior Prom to a mock accident-and-rescue to advertise the local Red Cross drive. Off campus, students can act out skits in front of the local supermarket to remind citizens to vote, to support the local Community Chest, or for some political purpose.

Guerrilla theater is a fanciful way for a person to show what he believes in by acting on his values. Done in the spirit of enlightenment, it can be informative without being offensive, and instructive without trampling on anyone's rights.

Footnotes

1. For the basic idea here I am indebted to Gail Koplow, Tufts University.

2. For the basic idea here I am indebted to Judy Wise, Fairleigh Dickinson University.

3. For further elaboration on this format, see Fannie R. Shaftel and George Shaftel, *Role Playing for Social Values,* Englewood Cliffs, N.J., Prentice-Hall, Inc., 1967.

4. This role play was developed by Dr. Jeffrey W. Eiseman, University of Massachusetts, Amherst.

5. Developed by Lois Jones, University of Massachusetts, Amherst.

6. For the notion of a decision agent I am indebted to H. B. Gelatt, College Entrance Examination Board.

7. Robert C. Hawley & Isabel L. Hawley, *A Handbook of Personal Growth Activities for Classroom Use,* Amherst, Mass., Education Research Associates, 1972, pp. 89-90.

8. *Ibid.,* p. 64.

Chapter Three:

TEACHING WITH ROLE PLAYING

The role play is but one of the many modes of teaching, along with the lecture, discussion, study and recitation, project work, and many others. It should not be thought of as a separate style of teaching, but rather as one more arrow in the teacher's quiver, to provide flexibility and variety in appropriate situations. The pedagogical structures and concerns discussed in this chapter apply not only to role playing but to many other areas of teaching as well.

The Sequence of Teaching Concerns

To use role play or any other teaching technique effectively, the teacher has first to create an atmosphere in the classroom which is conducive to mutual exchange and exploration. The following seven-part sequence of teaching concerns is designed to help teachers create the environment they want.[1] By focusing on one part of the sequence at a time, the teacher can plan for maximum effectiveness.

Orientation

The process of making the student feel comfortable, reducing his anxiety, and introducing him gradually to the situation at hand will liberate some of his intellectual energy which might otherwise be drained off by such questions as: Who is this teacher and what does he want from me? What can I do to stay out of trouble? How long will we have to be here? Where's the bathroom? What am I supposed to be doing?

Community Building

This is an extension of orientation. The more students can find in common with each other and with the teacher, the better they will be able to work together on a task. Community building is especially important for role playing or any other activity where the risks to individual self-esteem seem to be high.

Achievement Motivation

A further extension of orientation is for the teacher to set forth the goals of the class as he sees them, and to elicit from the students their goals. Students are likely to be better motivated when the goals, procedures, and rules of the class are clearly understood, and when the students have some voice in determining the goals, procedures, and rules. In particular, role playing is bound to be more successful if the students know why they are doing it. If, on the other hand, the teacher seems to be using role playing for some hidden objectives, the students will be distrustful, and hence less likely to participate enthusiastically.

Fostering Open Communication

As goals and objectives are clarified and as the class grows in its sense of community, then communication becomes more open and less subject to misunderstanding. In addition, the teacher can foster open communication by an attention to the physical arrangements in the room. Arranging the chairs in conversation units, in a circle or a semi-circle, and being sure that no one is sitting directly behind another person is one example; turning off a noisy air conditioner is another. If the teacher is to be the focus of class attention, he should avoid sitting in front of a glaring window. It is always surprising to me to notice how much a student's attention level drops off if his lines of communication—sight lines and sound lines—are not clear.

Information Seeking, Gathering, and Sharing

This is an extension of achievement motivation. In pursuing the goals and objectives of the class, what information is needed? What sources are available? What is the best way to gather the information and to disseminate it? Role playing almost invariably identifies information needs and often identifies resources as well. During the role play, the teacher should be listening carefully to determine information needs.

Value Exploration

From the gathering of information comes a need to organize the information, to determine which pieces are significant, which trivial. As information helps us to shape our values, so our values help us to determine the use that we make of information. During and after the role play, questions can be raised about what use we can make of material that we have elicited through the role play.

Planning for Change

Once we have helped students to explore their values and determined what things are important to them, then the final concern is to help the students plan for change. How can they make use of their learning experience? What alternative courses of action are open? What might be the consequences of each alternative? What specific behaviors and patterns can the individual student alter in order to become a more effective person?

A careful attention to these processes, and especially to the early steps—orientation, community building, and achievement motivation—will help to foster a sense of purpose and constructive behavior in the class.

Critical Thinking Skills: The Three-Step Watertight Compartments Model

I have found it useful to look at the critical thinking process in terms of three steps: gathering data, organizing data, and making use of data. In writing this book, for instance, the first step was to gather as much information about role playing and as many varieties of role-playing activities as possible—a great box full of odd slips of paper, notes, xeroxed pages, and earmarked books. The second step was to organize the information—sift through the box, sorting and arranging and sequencing, throwing away some, marking some as of special importance. The final step, making use of the data, was to determine the best way to display the organized data, to put it into final form for use—this book.

Students often try to organize and use their data before they have enough data collected in the first place. For instance, if a student is writing a composition on what he did during his summer vacation, his natural inclination is to start with pen and blank pieces of paper, trying to do all three steps at once: he tries to think what he did, how he should organize his experiences, and in what specific form he should put it down on paper—all at the same time. Naturally, he concludes that he really doesn't have anything to say.

On the other hand, if we use the watertight compartments model, the first step is for the teacher to ask him to brainstorm all the things he did during the summer (see Rules of Brainstorming, page 26). After he has amassed a large body of notes and ideas, then he is ready to organize—to look back over the collected data, gather similar items together, search for patterns, rank events in order of importance and draw some inferences. This leads naturally to the final compartment. When the data is organized and inferences have been drawn, then it is a relatively easy job to see how the data can best be used, in this case to fulfill an assignment for the composition teacher.

This three-step model of critical thinking has three important implications for role-playing:

First, a brainstorming approach can be useful to generate situations for role playing, to suggest possible alternatives to pursue in the role play, to list probable consequences of certain courses of action, to elicit conflict resolution plans, or to point up further information needs as felt by the group.

Second, the three-step model suggests that it is important to avoid jumping to conclusions on the basis of too little evidence. Even if the role play seemed very convincing, it should be kept in mind that other alternatives might yield other equally convincing solutions. In fact, the role play can be thought of as the first step in the three-step process: the more we can absorb of everything that is going on during the role play, the more useful information we are likely to have in hand when the role play is over. After the role play, some attempt should be made to organize the information and draw inferences from it before jumping to conclusions as to what we should or should not do as a result of our investigation.

Finally, the third step, making use of the data, is one which is too often omitted in role-play sessions. I feel strongly that time should be allowed after every role-play session to formulate proposals for changes in attitudes and behaviors: *What did this all mean anyway, and how can I use it to become a more effective person?*

Brainstorming

In the Decisions Role Play described in Chapter One, the teacher asked the class to brainstorm for four minutes on the topic of what decisions Sue might have to make during the next year of her life. The lists that was generated included such widely different items as *nose surgery, abortion,* and *la-*

crosse practice. Cutting hair was "piggybacked" by someone who said *cutting class* and by someone who added *having ears pierced.* And there was no negative evaluation when items that may have seemed to be outside the category of decisions, such as *dates, driving,* or *acne,* were mentioned. Thus, the class generated a long list of decisions which included many items of real concern to the students.

During a role play, when one character seems to be stuck or unable to determine a course of action, the teacher might ask the entire class to brainstorm responses, thus providing a large body of material for the character to draw on.

After the role play, the class can brainstorm information needs, possible alternatives to the course of action that the role play took, or possible no-lose resolutions to the conflict.

The Six-Part Valuing Process

A useful framework for organizing a post-role-play discussion is the six-part valuing process, first formulated by Louis Raths.[2] The first four parts deal with choosing a value, the last two deal with acting on the value:

1. IDENTIFYING PREFERENCES: What do I really like? What do I want? What can make me happy?

2. IDENTIFYING INFLUENCES: What influences have led me to these preferences? How much is my choice determined by my parents, by my peers, by the subtle pressures of the media? How freely have I chosen?

3. IDENTIFYING ALTERNATIVES: What are the possible alternatives to this choice? Have I given sufficient consideration to these alternatives?

4. IDENTIFYING CONSEQUENCES: What are the probable and possible consequences for each alternative? Am I willing to risk the consequences? Are the consequences socially beneficial or socially harmful?

5. ACTING: Am I able to act on the choices I have made? How do my actions reflect my choice?

6. PATTERNING: Do my actions reflect a continuing commitment to this choice? How can I change the patterns of my life so that this choice is continually reflected in my actions?

As the teacher listens to the role play, he may become aware of the expression of preferences, the identification of influences, the search for alternatives, and the eliciting of probable and possible consequences. He may also notice some planning for action and identify possible ways of patterning. When the teacher hears some of these areas being touched upon in the role play, he might jot down notes to use for later reference in the post-role-play discussion.

Clarifying Questions for Use in Post-Role-Play Discussion

Several of the clarifying questions in this list are based directly on the six-part valuing scheme above.

1. What alternatives did the players consider?

2. Can you think of some alternatives that were not considered?

3. What would be the probable consequences of the line of action that was being taken?

4. What risks were involved?

5. What would you consider a satisfactory outcome at this point?

6. Would both parties consider this a satisfactory outcome?

7. What is the probability for a satisfactory outcome at this point?

8. What kind of relationship did you hear being portrayed?

9. How well did the players define the problem?

10. Did you hear some hidden messages being passed?

11. How would you characterize the communication that took place?

12. Did the discussion shift to the personalities of the individuals, or did it concentrate on the problem?

13. Were there some assumptions made by either of the individuals about the other that might not be justified?

14. What are some of the influences that might have led these people to act in the way that they have?

15. How clear are their objectives? Do you think that they have some objectives that even they don't understand very well? What are these?

Nine Cautions

1. I've found it best to proceed on the assumption that there are no "wrong answers"; that is, that any response within the role play or after it may be valuable for study. Avoid commenting on the authenticity of a role play or on the appropriateness of any response. Consider all the material elicited as useful for analysis, even that which seems "phony." *Why was it phony?* is a good point for discussion. Have faith in the class to correct its own deficiencies. Students will be sure to police one another on the point of realism or of logic. (But don't let them interrupt the role play in progress to offer negative criticism.)

2. Avoid as much as possible the slightest semblance of a hidden agenda in terms of the outcome or "lesson" to be learned from the role play. If the students sense that you're out to teach them that Sue should realize that she's too young and immature to go to the concert, or that "honesty is the best policy," then they will make nice noises to please the teacher on that point (or perversely, they will bring up all the special cases where honesty doesn't pay so as to cloud the whole issue).

3. Avoid overdirecting. Let the role players move in their own direction, even if that direction

seems to be at odds from the objectives you had planned for the lesson. (Remember, the role play need last only three to five minutes.)

4.　Remember that role playing is not a theatrical situation—there should be no criticism of acting ability.

5.　Frequently announce the "right to pass." Every student should have the right to decline to take part or share his views at any time, including all the time.

6.　Avoid confronting an individual with a level of risk which is too high for him. One of the strengths of the open-chair technique is that it lowers the risk level to participants. I strongly believe that no one should be appointed or "volunteered" or urged to take a role. The individual knows best what's best for him.

7.　Avoid putting an individual on the spot concerning his views. "Do you *really* feel that way?" or "How can you defend that position?" or "You can't really be serious about that?" can all be very damaging to a weak ego. Appropriate ways to probe further would be, "Can you tell us more about that?" or "Would you like to go into that?" or "Do you want to add anything to that?"

8. Be careful not to focus too narrowly on predetermined teaching objectives, such as the five-step model of decision-making or identifying specific communication skills. It is important to have learning objectives in mind for role playing, but the medium is so powerful that often a more important or more meaningful path to discovery will be opened than the teacher had thought of. Students are very good judges of this. If they find an area to explore that is outside the objectives that you have set down, then the new area is probably meaningful to them, and worth spending some time with.

9. And finally, don't beat a dead horse. Much of the learning that takes place in role playing is tacit, private and individual. The fact that an individual doesn't respond in a given way to a teacher's question is no indication that he hasn't learned anything.

Evaluating Role-Playing Sessions

The two forms which follow are provided to help evaluate role playing sessions:

The *Teacher Self-Evaluation Form* is designed for teachers who wish to use a structured approach to self-evaluation. Generally, the form should be completed as soon after the session as possible.

Some teachers have found it useful to collect self-evaluation forms and review them at regular intervals: monthly, for instance, or at the end of a unit.

The *Student Feedback Form* is an important instrument for three reasons: First, it gives the teacher a chance to check his own perceptions of the class against those of the students. Second, student feedback is often helpful in identifying student needs for future planning. And third, when the teacher collects student feedback and uses student ideas in lesson planning, students begin to feel that they can have some influence over their learning situation, and thus can begin to recognize and accept their own responsibility for their education.

While the systematic collection of self-evaluation and feedback is an important part of improving teaching skills, these forms represent only one variety of each. Other self-evaluation methods include anecdotal records, teaching journals, incidental notes collected in a folder, and audio or video taping of sessions. For student feedback, letters to the teacher, student journals, thought cards, or a suggestion box can be used.

Teacher Self-Evaluation Form

1. Did the members of the class seem to understand my objectives?

2. Was I able to elicit objectives from the members of the class and incorporate them into the lesson?

3. Circle one number on each of the following continuums to indicate an overall impression of the classroom behavior:

1	2	3	4	5	6	7
PURPOSEFUL						FRIVOLOUS

1	2	3	4	5	6	7
SPIRITED						SOLEMN

1	2	3	4	5	6	7
FRIENDLY						HOSTILE

4. Jot down a sentence or two about what you felt were the best features of the class.

5. What would you like to change before role playing in this way again?

6. Open comment:

Student Feedback Form

1. Was the session interesting to you?

2. What did you learn from the session?

3. Circle one number on each of the following continuums to indicate an overall impression of the classroom behavior:

1		3	4	5	6	7
PURPOSEFUL						FRIVOLOUS

1	2	3	4	5	6	7
SPIRITED						SOLEMN

1	2	3	4	5	6	7
FRIENDLY						HOSTILE

4. What were the best features of this session?

5. What things could be changed to make these sessions better for you?

6. What things could you do for yourself to help make these sessions better for you?

7. Open comment:

. . . .

NAME (optional)

Footnotes

1. For a full discussion of this sequence of teaching concerns and many suggestions for its implementation in the classroom, see Robert C. Hawley, *Human Values in the Classroom*, Amherst, Mass., Education Research Associates, 1973.

2. The following is an adaptation by Robert C. Hawley and David D. Britton of the seven valuing criteria presented in Louis Raths, et. al., *Values and Teaching*, Columbus, Ohio, Charles E. Merrill, 1966.

Chapter Four

THE USES OF ROLE PLAYING

The benefits that can be derived from role playing can be viewed in terms of five general and over-lapping categories: problem solving, rehearsing, reporting, developing empathy, and managing the class. Because role playing is so versatile and broad in its scope, the teacher will often be able to accomplish two or three of these objectives at the same time.

The Decisions Role Play outlined in Chapter One was designed primarily to teach problem solving: identifying patterns of problem solving by the individual and by the group, seeking alternatives, examining consequences, exploring the interpersonal factors that go into problem solving.

The Decisions Role Play can also be of aid in rehearsing or trying out a behavior. For example, if there had been a real Sue in the class who was about to confront her father with a similar request, the role play would have made her more aware of the possibilities in the situation. Rehearsing is also useful to help identity formation and to explore self-concepts by comparing one's real self with the self that one is rehearsing.

Role playing can be used effectively for reporting—reenacting or reconstructing a situation from the experience of the students, or from literature or history. Rather than *telling* about the event, the players can *show* what happened in the cafeteria, in the story, or in the history book.

The ability to empathize permits the student to see a social act from the perspectives of others who might be affected by that act; thus the student acquires a wider view of the impact and the consequences of the act. When a student is put into the role of a person under some stressful situation, he may be able to see more clearly what might cause that person to act as he does. In the case of the role play in Chapter One, the students playing Dad, and possibly those watching, may get a clearer notion of how a father feels when put in that position. It is this ability to empathize that is often considered the basis for moral and ethical judgment.

And finally, through role playing the teacher can often accomplish many of the tasks of managing the class: building a cohesive and supportive group, diagnosing the needs of students, evaluating the amount of information that has been acquired, motivating the class to higher achievement, and modifying socially unacceptable behavior. Role playing can turn a mirror on the class so that individuals can see the significance of their actions in the light of their relationship to the entire class.

These five broad uses of role playing will be broken down into specific objectives in order to help clarify the multiple purposes of role playing, and to give the teacher some help in working up lesson plans and statements of objectives. Once again, however, it is important to stress that even a very short role play will encompass a wide variety of these objectives; for the teacher to focus too narrowly on one or two objectives may cause students to miss significant learning opportunities that are outside the specific objectives of the lesson.

Problem-Solving Objectives

1. *To help students to identify the real problem.*   Often, when there is a decision to be made or a conflict to be resolved, the most difficult part of the process is to determine exactly what is the nature of the conflict or the seat of conflict. For instance, in the Sue and Dad role play in Chapter One, what is the real problem: how to get Dad to let Sue go to the concert, how to get Sue and Jim together, how to determine which decisions Sue is mature enough to make on her own? Or is there a deeper underlying problem in the relationship between Sue and Dad?

2. *To help students see that behavior is purposive.* Most behavior is goal-directed. Role playing can help to show the link between behavior and its goals so that students can become more able to see the goal of a given behavior. Thus, they can better evaluate whether or not the behavior is an effective means of achieving the goal, and, more important, whether the goal is appropriate in the situation or acceptable to society. What are Sue's real goals in wanting to go to the concert?

3. *To help each student to explore and clarify his own frame of values.* Values are the principles upon which decision making is based. By responding in concrete situations where decisions have to be made, and by watching others respond to those situations, each student can become more aware of his own frame of reference in valuing.

4. *To help students test their values through simulated action.* As students engage in role playing and watch others role play, they can see the effects of their choices in action.

5. *To help students realize that their decisions have consequences.* As students see the effects of their choices and of the choices of others in role-playing situations, they may come to have a

greater awareness that consequences inevitably follow from their decisions.

6. *To help students enlarge their problem-solving capability through the habit of seeking alternatives.* As students see each other work out solutions to problems, they come to see a wide variety of alternatives brought into play. This expands their own reservoir of possible alternatives. In addition, by consciously generating several alternatives before deciding on a solution to a role-play problem, students increase their capability in generating useful alternatives in their daily lives.

7. *To help students identify the underlying influences in decision making.* The more fully aware a person is of the influences that bear upon him, the more independent he can be in making his decision. Role playing is an excellent tool to highlight the hidden influences of peer pressure, for example, or of the hidden commandments of the family, of an ethnic group, or of television advertising.

8. *To confront and evaluate the ways in which we tend to solve interpersonal problems.* People often put off formal decision making, hoping that somehow they can muddle through. Role playing often demonstrates to students that the consequences of avoiding a problem are a loss of op-

tions and a reduction in personal effectiveness. Students are thus in a better position to evaluate just when is the right time to take steps to confront their problems.

9. *To demonstrate the effectiveness of group problem solving.* Most personal problems are, in fact, interpersonal—that is, they bear on more than one person. In these situations, the added perspective that several people can bring to the problem often increases the chances of arriving at an effective solution. The superiority of a group approach to problem solving in certain situations has been amply demonstrated. Role playing can give students the chance to see group problem solving in action, and to evaluate its potential effectiveness for them.

10. *To help students distinguish between the overt demand and the underlying desire in interpersonal conflict situations.* Sue's overt demand is to be permitted to go to the concert, but her underlying desire may be to be with Jim. Dad's overt demand is that Sue stay home, but his underlying desire may be that she not place herself in a dangerous situation where she may get hurt. The overt demands are in direct conflict, but the underlying desires are not necessarily in conflict. Role playing provides the opportunity to observe and dissect conflict situations so that students can see the un-

derlying desires clearly and put conflict resolution techniques into action.

11. *To demonstrate the necessity of open communication in problem solving.* Interpersonal conflict can often be seen as a breakdown in communication. In a case where individuals communicate their overt demands but fail to communicate their underlying desires, the underlying desires can be seen as the hidden agenda of the conflict. Role playing is an effective way to examine interpersonal communication and distinguish the surface message from the hidden message.

Rehearsing Objectives

1. *To rehearse or simulate specific situations in order to be more aware of the behavioral possibilities contained within the situations.* The classic example is the role play of a job interview or a college admissions interview. Rehearsing gives the student an experiential awareness of what may be involved in a new or potentially threatening situation; thus, students have a chance to better prepare for the situation and lessen their anxiety. This kind of rehearsing is most effective when the "interviewer" has specific knowledge of the situation either through actual experience or through obser-

vation or research. Students who have just come back from a college interview might play the interviewer, for instance.

2. *To help students become more aware of their own identity by seeing themselves reflected in the mirror of the group.* The process of identity formation involves observing one's own actions and reactions and comparing these with the actions and reactions of others. In this way, the individual can identify his own uniqueness. Role playing gives a special opportunity to observe the behavior of others in a given situation, and to compare that behavior with one's own anticipated behavior in the same situation.

3. *To help students to gain self-control through self-knowledge.* The major thrust of modern clinical psychology indicates that self-knowledge is the major path to self-improvement and self-control. Role playing provides a unique opportunity for the student to become more aware of his patterns of feeling, thinking, and acting.

4. *To help students to become self-motivated through self-awareness.* Recent studies indicate that students with healthy and positive self-concepts show significantly more motivation toward academic achievement than do students with poorly

defined and/or negative self-concepts (see especially Schmuck and Schmuck, *Group Processes in the Classroom,* 1971). Through its rehearsing of real life situations, role playing provides the opportunity for students to define and improve their self-concepts and thus to increase their self-motivation.

Reporting Objectives

1. *To report on an interview or action project.* When students are sent in teams of two or three to interview members of the community, the corner policeman, or shoppers at the local supermarket, for instance, their report to the rest of the class can be cast in the form of a role play.

2. *To report on a personal problem.* In counseling situations, an individual can report on his internal conflict with another by role playing the situation before the group—either by playing both parts himself or by engaging a helper to play the other part.

3. *To report interpersonal conflicts.* An intriguing use of role playing (reported in Dreikurs, *Maintaining Sanity in the Classroom,* 1971) is in settling elementary school playground disturbances. When the two combatants come before the

teacher, each complaining that the other started it, the teacher asks them to *show,* not just tell, what happened. As the students act out what they think was the beginning of the conflict, the situation is generally clarified. The students see the source of the conflict, and often the teacher has little more to do.

4. *To give a book report or a report on a project in history or current events.* Rather than telling about the book or the event, the reporters can describe the overall situation and then do a brief role play of one of the events. This works best when two or three students are making a joint report on the same book or event.

Empathy-Developing Objectives

1. *To help students to develop social competence in judgment and action by giving them the viewpoints of others in a social context.* The students who play "Dad" in the Decisions Role Play in Chapter One, for instance, are almost certain to have a broader insight into the specific problems of parenthood by being forced to try to think as a parent would think. And the observers, too, by witnessing the tension between the role of Dad and the real life of the students playing Dad, become more

aware of the way a parent may think and feel in such a situation. The more a person is aware of the thinking and feeling of others, the more likely it is that he will include this information in his frame of reference for deciding. This wider viewpoint helps to clarify the lines of communication and to reduce unintentional conflict.

2. *To develop a tolerance for the behavior and motivation of others.* The more a person is able to put himself in the situation of another, the more he will be able to see the motivation behind that person's action. Thus, a person who has played Dad, even though he might not agree with him, will be more likely to understand why Dad tends to avoid the real issues in the situation.

3. *To develop in students the ability to make moral judgments on the basis of a more comprehensive view of the situation.* According to Lawrence Kohlberg's theory, the principal factor in promoting the development of the moral faculties of children is the taking of a wide variety of social roles, a process that Kohlberg calls role taking. Because the child who has engaged in many roles knows how it feels to be a teacher, student, dishwasher, cookie server, lemonade seller, etc., the child can appreciate the moral question from positions other than the one he is in at the moment. The child who has

been a cookie server, for instance, knows the responsibility involved in cookie service and is likely to take this into account before deciding whether or not to swipe an extra cookie when somebody else is the cookie server. Role playing is a vicarious form of role taking in which young people can simulate various social roles and thus develop their moral reasoning.

Classroom-Managing Objectives

1. *To develop a sense of community in the classroom.* Recent research indicates the importance of community in achieving the academic goals of the class (see Schmuck and Schmuck, 1971). Role playing is one method of developing a sense of community within the classroom. As students see and hear each other role play situations, they can compare how they might react in a similar circumstance and thus come to understand each other better.

2. *To help overcome specific problems in group dynamics in the classroom.* Problems such as newcomers to the class, the rejection of one or more members of the class by others, and the problem of cliques can be explored and relieved by the careful use of role playing. In Chapter Two, there

are several role playing formats which can be used to deal with problems in this area.

3. *To provide for open and supportive communication in the classroom.* By focusing on aspects of communication and identifying such blocks to open communication as sarcasm and put-downs, role playing can help students learn how to develop more productive methods of communication.

4. *To diagnose the informational needs of the students.* Role-playing situations which parallel the experience of students may help the teacher to identify the students' specific needs. The way a high school senior in a role play reacts to questions posed by a college interviewer may tell us much about the student's needs for information and/or clarification of life goals.

5. *To evaluate the progress of the class in terms of the acquisition of new information.* Role playing a specific situation derived from a unit of study can help the teacher to determine how much new information the students have absorbed on the subject. For instance, if a situation from history is being role played, the teacher can assess the degree to which students have retained and understood the historical facts and concepts of the period. Using role play in a drug education class, the teacher

can evaluate the level of information present which is being enlisted in the decision-making process. And in teaching formal decision making, the teacher can determine how well students have acquired a framework for decision making—searching for alternatives, checking consequences, being aware of problem-centering and person-centering, and so forth.

6. *To help motivate the student toward achieving the goals of the class.*   A brief role play followed by a discussion focusing on what issues in the role play interest the students can help the teacher to plan the subject-area unit to take into account student needs. Before the class reads *The Iliad,* for instance, there could be a brief role play between father and son in which the father takes back the car that he has given to his son because the father has smashed his own car beyond repair.

Chapter Five

WHAT TO DO WHEN THINGS GO WRONG

The class has just completed a brief role play. You, the teacher, are about to ask for comments when Susan, a member of the class, says, "This is stupid. Why don't we get back to doing our regular work?"

What do you say?

1. "Well, Susan, I'm sorry you feel that way. Suppose you tell the class just exactly what you feel is stupid about the role play."

2. "The educational literature has many references to the use of role playing as a legitimate teaching technique. Let us continue."

3. "I was only using role playing to liven up the class. I certainly hope that most of you appreciate that."

4. "No one technique is equally suited to everybody, and role playing may not

> be for you. But I'd like you to see if you
> can follow along and find some value in
> this exercise."

5. "Thank you for speaking up. How do
   others of you feel about it?"

Although I have probably used variations of
all of the five choices above at one time or another,
upon reflection, I would like to reject choices one,
two, and three, and advocate either four or five.

Choices one and two provoke Susan to raise her
defenses. The first choice puts her on the spot,
forces her to come up with points which the teacher
may very likely shoot down. The second, an appeal
to a higher authority, shows up the student as being
ignorant or uninitiated. The third response is be-
littling to the educational process: role playing *is* a
way to liven up the class, but it is more than just
an amusement to fill up class time.

On the other hand, the fourth response recognizes the legitimacy of individual differences, and
it includes an appeal for Susan to expand her range
of acceptance for different ideas and new ways of
doing things. The fifth response indicates that the
teaching and learning process is a suitable area for
classroom discussion. With any luck, the discussion
will help the teacher to gain a fresh perspective on
the needs and desires of students, while at the same

time the students will develop a clearer insight into the problems of teaching.

Typical Classroom Problems

Because every classroom group is unique and has a character of its own, it is hard to generalize about specific classroom problems. Usually, the advice is either too specific and therefore not appropriate to a different situation, or so general that there is no way to apply the advice to specific cases. With this disclaimer in mind, I would like to put forth some additional classroom problems and suggest ways of resolving them.

Unconventional Views

Classes occasionally contain one or two individuals who make it a practice to express unconventional viewpoints. The presence of such students often leads to an undercurrent of guerrilla warfare between the iconoclasts and the supporters of conventional wisdom. This conflict may very well show up in role playing. Let us say, for instance, that the class is involved in a role play about the issue of amnesty for Vietnam war deserters and draft evaders. One of the role players suggests that all of the deserters should be brought home and given color television sets and new automobiles as an expression of good will from the American people at large. Another student breaks in and says, "Aw, come on, be serious. You're always saying things like that. Everyone knows that's stupid. Why don't you try to be more realistic?"

What should the teacher do?

In the first place, it is important to offer protection to an individual who takes a strong position on a controversial matter. But on the other hand, the teacher should avoid the natural temptation to put down the putdowner, since one teaches as much by example as by precept. In addition, the person who has expressed the unconventional view may be motivated by the need to draw attention to himself rather than from any real belief in what he is saying. Anything the teacher says or does should take these various factors into account. Here's a possible response:

Let's remember that, as usual in this class, we're operating in the spirit of brainstorming: all ideas are encouraged, even those which may seem wildly unrealistic. Furthermore, let's not confuse the role with the player. In role playing, the views that you express don't have to be your own, although they can be. I think it's useful to have ideas expressed that are uncommon or unusual just so that we can test these against the more usual ideas."

In this response, the teacher re-establishes the

nonjudgmental, nonevaluative norm of brainstorming as a mode of inquiry. Furthermore, the teacher casts the conflict in terms of ideas rather that individuals. By doing so, the teacher reinforces the principle that individuals in this classroom are unconditionally valued for being themselves—not conditionally valued for what they say or do.

Discussion Killers

Occasionally a student will make a comment that will effectively kill the discussion—a comment that no one cares to expand upon or differ with. When this happens and the discussion suddenly goes dead, it's probably best not to try to revive the discussion, but rather to move to a new area. The Clarifying Questions for Use in Post-Role-Play Discussions (see page 117) are often useful as starting points for refocusing a discussion after it has been killed.

Off the Subject

This is a tricky question: When is the discussion "off the subject"? In role playing and the post-role-play discussion, there are so many areas for fruitful inquiry that it is often difficult to say precisely what the subject is, and thus when the discussion is "off." The teacher who leads a discussion along a predetermined course runs the risk of losing both student interest and student response. Yet it is undeniable that a free discussion can easily dissipate into mouthing vague generalizations and easy platitudes.

One method for dealing with this situation is to write on the board a list of questions relating to the topic. These can be predetermined by the teacher or brainstormed by the whole class. Then as the discussion moves along, the teacher can test its relevance by asking, "Which one of the questions on the board does this discussion pertain to, or does it pertain to another question that we should have up on the board?"

Another method is to consult the class:

"One of my stated objectives in holding this discussion was to get at several alternative courses of action or attitude, and to think through the consequences of these alternatives. We seem to be getting away from that objective. Do you think we should refocus the discussion, or is it meaningful to you as it has developed thus far?"

A third method to help prevent straying from the main subject is to designate one or two students as "content observers" who will follow the discussion with an eye to seeing its logical development. These observers could then be called upon to describe the course of the discussion, including the question of whether the class has moved off the subject.

Can't Get Started

Sometimes at the beginning of a role play the players find difficulty in starting—they hem and giggle, squirm and smile. Here the teacher might say the following:

"This seems to be a hard one to get started. Let's everybody brainstorm for a minute or two on what either of these two roles might say to get started in this situation." After the class has provided five or ten openers, the teacher could halt the brainstorming and ask the role players to pick one of the suggestions as a starting point.

Nobody Volunteers

If nobody volunteers for a role play (a situation which almost never happens) the teacher can simply assign half the class to play each role. Then if the sides have trouble getting started, brainstorming can be used as in the above example.

Only One Volunteer

If only one person volunteers for a role which was to be played by the multiple-parts technique, the teacher might do a little coaxing: "Come on, who will be good enough to help Billy out with this role?" If there are still no further volunteers, the teacher should give the single volunteer every opportunity to withdraw, since he volunteered in the belief that there would be others to help out. Then the situation can be handled as in the case of no volunteers (above).

Group Too Small for Multiple Parts

When working with a group of six to ten where there would be very few observers left if two or three people played each part, the group can be divided as above and each half take on a role.

Same Volunteers

A pattern sometimes develops in which the same few students volunteer each time. To encourage wider participation, the teacher might say:

"Let's give the first shot to those who haven't had a chance to play a role yet. All those who have played a role keep your hands down for now. Anyone who has not, but would now like to, raise your hand."

Then the teacher should be prepared to wait in silence for several seconds so that the more reticent students will have a chance to volunteer.

Side Conversations

Side conversations develop not only in role playing, but also in other classroom situations. Since these conversations often pertain to the topic at hand, I prefer not to disturb them if they are not distracting to the group.

Side conversations generally develop because students are having trouble seeing or hearing what's going on, and lose touch with the main discussion. The more that the teacher can improve the physical arrangement of the classroom so that all students can have eye contact, the less likely that nonrelevant side conversations will develop.

Silliness, Horsing Around

When there is general silliness or horsing around, this could be a sign that the material under discussion is not relevant to the lives of the students. On the other hand, with the highly personal content that role playing often elicits, horseplay may be a sign that the content is too personal, that the students are having trouble coming to grips with it. The teacher might address the class in the following manner:

"For some reason you don't seem to be able to deal with the topic at hand. I'm not sure whether this is because the topic is not relevant to you or because it is too close to your personal lives, or some other reason. Would you take a minute to jot down notes to yourself as to why we are having this difficulty? Then I would like to have a discussion on this problem for a few minutes."

A third possible reason for horseplay and silliness is that the students may have an overabundance of physical energy—arising, for instance, from the feeling of release after a big test the period before. Here some kind of tension-releasing activity or physical game may be called for, such as *Adverbs* or ——*ly* (see pages 97 and 98).

Withdrawal

Teachers are sometimes concerned over a student who seems to withdraw, or one who, while not an introvert, takes no part in the discussion or activities. As with side conversations, those who withdraw may be doing so because they are physically out of touch with the main group, unable to see or hear clearly. On the other hand, withdrawing is one form of "passing," and although the student should be provided with every opportunity to enter into the activity of the group, in the last analysis the student's right to pass must be honored.

One Student Exposes Self More Than He/She Intended

Especially where personal issues are involved, there is always the remote chance that a student will get too deeply involved in a role, expose more of himself or herself than he or she intended, and later regret this. The teacher who is aware of this possibility can cut the role play before such a level is reached. If this is not possible, the teacher should be sure to give the student every opportunity to talk about his or her feelings in the post-role-play discussion; the teacher should also be on hand, if possible, after class for advice and consultation.

Can't Get Out of Role, or Can't Discuss Objectively

In a role play of genuine controversy, such as the issue of women's rights, a player might get into such an argumentative state that he or she finds it difficult to be objective in the post-role-play discussion. Here is a good place for role reversal. Ask the participants to adopt the other side of the issue and repeat the role play for a minute or two. (Having the students reverse their physical location helps them to take on the new role.)

After this role reversal, the teacher should try to elicit statements from the students on their feelings about being placed in the new perspective. The effectiveness of role reversal lies not only in the cognitive awareness of the arguments on the other side, but also in the awareness of the *feelings* of those who stand for another point of view.

Almost all of the problems connected with teaching and learning should be open for student exploration. When the teacher views his or her role as a facilitator, a coordinator, and a provider of learning experiences, then the question of "what to do when things go wrong" becomes one for the whole class to share in; it is no longer a burden for the teacher alone. The more the students can be involved in helping to analyze and solve these problems, the more they will realize their ultimate responsibility for their own learning.

Chapter Six

ROLE PLAYING AND THE DEVELOPMENT OF MORAL JUDGMENT

The work of Lawrence Kohlberg is of immense importance for teachers concerned with developing techniques for moral education. Kohlberg's researches have led him to reject what he calls the "bag of virtues" technique for moral education, in which the student is drilled in honesty, responsibility, fairness, acceptance of others, and so forth. Instead, Kohlberg believes that the child develops moral judgment (and thus moral behavior) through six successive stages of knowing and understanding the world.

This cognitive developmental process is not facilitated by rote learning of a list of *shoulds* and *shouldn'ts*. What the child needs is a continuous exposure to new and changing perspectives concerning the individual's relationship to other individuals, and to his society. The more aware a person is of the potential impact of his actions on others, and the more he is able to empathize with others, the more information he will have upon which to base a moral judgment. The potential bicycle thief who has himself struggled to earn money to buy a bicycle is more likely to consider the feelings of his potential victim.

The crucial factor in the development of moral judgment is what Kohlberg calls "role taking"—that is, taking part in the workings of society in many different social roles—orange juice server, blackboard eraser, student, teacher, buyer, seller, and so forth. The quality of an education for moral judgment is directly related to the number of opportunities that are provided for role taking, and to the quality of the available roles. Thus a kindergarten where children serve the juice, lead the Pledge of Allegiance, take a variety of leader and follower roles in games, and have several learning opportunities to choose from at any one time is conducive to the development of moral judgment. On the other hand, a kindergarten where all leadership and direction come from the teacher, and where the children are instructed to sit with hands folded while, for example, individuals go to the bathroom one by one, does not aid the development of moral judgment. The first kindergarten not only has more potential roles for children to assume, it also has roles that involve leadership, decision making, and relationships of trust and responsibility.

The Stages of Moral Development

As the child perceives and reflects on how his actions affect others and how others' actions affect him, he constructs a set of ethical principles to govern his behavior in interpersonal and social situations. These principles form a definition of justice and equality which changes and grows more comprehensive as the child moves through different stages of moral development. Thus, children progress in their moral development in much the same way that Piaget suggests children progress in their cognitive development. Kohlberg postulates six stages of moral development:

One: Punishment and Obedience Orientation

The young child with his limited experience defines moral situations in terms of authority and power. He thinks in clear terms of right or wrong, good or bad, based on the weight of external authority whose claim to justice is raw power. "Mother wants me to finish my milk and therefore finishing my milk is the right thing to do." Avoidance of punishment and obedience to power are valued in their own right.

Two: Instrumental Relativist Orientation

As the child grows in his knowledge of the world, he begins to see right action as that which will meet his own needs. Fairness and reciprocity come in as a direct, physical exchange: "I want the toy you're playing with so I'll give you a toy of mine." Or conversely, "You hurt me, so it is fair that I should hurt you."

Three: Interpersonal Concordance, or "Good Boy —Nice Girl," Orientation

As notions of reciprocity and fairness grow, the individual thinks more in terms of acquiring "points" in exchange for favors: "I'll be good so that you will take me to the circus." It becomes important to earn approval for being "nice" or for conforming to the expectations of those whom one values.

These first three stages are all "I-Thou"— strictly interpersonal in context. The concepts of society and social order have not yet appeared. As the individual gains experience in social situations· where society becomes an entity in his thinking, he begins to make moral decisions on the basis of the "goodness" or "badness" of the action in relation to society. Again, the progression through the stages of moral development is determined by the individual's expanding awareness, based on expanding experiences.

Four: Law and Order Orientation

At this stage, there is an orientation toward

maintaining the social order: "Laws exist to protect society and we should do our duty and obey the law to preserve the established order."

Five: Utilitarian Social Contract Orientation

At stage five, moral action is based upon the principles of the social order. Social justice is defined by a set of principles which have evolved through history and which have been tacitly agreed upon by the whole society. "Laws were made for the benefit of all men. Where laws no longer fit our needs we may change them, but we should work within the system for change."

Six: Universal Ethical Principle Orientation

At the final stage, the individual sees moral justice as an obligation to his conscience based upon self-chosen ethical principles which are logical, universal, and consistent. These principles are based on a respect for the dignity of human beings as individual persons—as ends in themselves rather than as means to ends.

An individual must pass through each stage in turn before reaching a higher one—no skipping is possible. Generally, an individual can understand the logic of moral principles one stage above his own stage of growth, but he will fail to comprehend an argument presented to him at more than one stage above his present level. This means that an attempt to teach notions of the social contract, for instance, to children who are at Stage Two or Three will be unsuccessful: the children lack the cognitive tools to understand or use the concept.

However, if the teaching is only one stage above the present level of the student, the student is attracted to that more advanced logic and will begin to adopt it for his own, thus moving toward the next stage of moral development.

From this perception, Kohlberg proposes that the way to help students with the development of moral judgment is to test their present level and then to hold discussions on moral issues, presenting arguments one stage above the level of the students. Several of Kohlberg's associates have demonstrated a limited amount of success with this method. Unfortunately, testing the stage of moral development of students is difficult and time-consuming, and furthermore, the students in any one class tend to be at two or three different stages.

In one early study, a class of children who were predominantly Stage Two's and Three's was conducted by a teacher who provided arguments at Stage Four. The class held open discussions of moral issues, with the Stage Three students expected to influence the Stage Two students, and the teacher expected to influence the Stage Three students. The results indicated that the Stage Two students learned from their Stage Three peers and moved toward Stage Three, while the teacher was less effective in promoting growth of the Stage Three students toward Stage Four.

This study suggests that having students engage in dicussion of moral issues with other students will probably be beneficial even when no attempt is made to assess the specific developmental levels of the members of the class. The discussion will likely be worthwhile because a variety of levels is almost sure to be represented, and because students seem to make the best moral teachers.

Role playing fits into this scheme in two ways: First, it is a method for holding vivid, intensive discussions on moral issues. Rather than talk about whether or not a man should steal in an attempt to save his wife's life, the situation can be role played between the man and the intended robbery victim. The wife could be brought in as a third role.

Second, role playing provides a kind of vicarious role taking, and thereby provides a chance to gain in the ability to empathize with persons in similar roles.

In contriving problems and dilemmas for promoting moral development through role playing, I have found useful a listing of issues based on those developed by Kohlberg for research purposes. My list includes the following areas of concern:

> Life.
>
> Property.
>
> Civil rights (liberty).
>
> Public welfare.
>
> Truth and trust.
>
> Love.
>
> Punishment and the legal system.
>
> Family and friendship.
>
> Citizenship and authority.

In selecting the Life issue or the Property issue, for instance, the attempt is not to teach a single virtue such as the dignity of life or the right to individual property. Rather, these broad issues are useful as poles around which to weave specific problems that will engage the student in moral probing and decision making.

The following is a series of moral problems and dilemmas suitable for role playing. I prefer to use these as open-chair role plays, that is, asking two or three individuals to play each role or dividing the room in half and asking each half to play a role.

These problems can also be played by individuals, and they can be used for multiple role playing (see pp. 80-84) or for written role playing (see pp. 101-102).

The Tibetan Monk

In a decrepit monastery high in the mountains of far-off Tibet, there sits an ancient monk in a narrow cell. He is the source of all worldly ills. You have it within your power to press a single button on your desk and thereby destroy the monk. This act will release the entire world from its misery of human suffering, from wars and famine and pestilence. Will you press the button?

Role play two individuals seated with the button between them. One wants to press the button. The other wants to talk him out of it.

The Heinz Dilemma[1]

In a certain town in Europe, a woman is dying from a rare form of cancer. The doctors have little hope for her, except for the possibility of one drug which has recently been developed by a chemist in that town. The drug cost the chemist $200 to make, but he is charging $2,000 to purchase it. Heinz, the sick woman's husband, cannot afford the drug. He tries to borrow money from everyone he knows, but he can raise only $1,000. He asks the chemist to let him have the drug for less money or to let him pay for it later, but the chemist refuses. Heinz considers breaking into the chemist's laboratory to steal the drug.

Role play the two halves of Heinz—one wanting to steal the drug, the other not wanting to. Or role play Heinz and the druggist, Heinz trying to persuade the druggist to take less money. Add Heinz's wife.

Extensions

1.   Heinz steals the drug and is caught. Role play Heinz and the judge whose court is trying Heinz.

2.   The drug doesn't work. In agony, Heinz's wife asks the doctor to kill her and end her misery. The doctor does, but he is caught. Role play the doctor and the judge.

3.   Heinz is sent to jail for stealing the drug. He escapes, settles in another town, and lives there as a model citizen, devoting his spare time and energies to local charity work. One day, five years later, the judge who tried Heinz visits the town. He sees Heinz and recognizes him as the escaped convict. He makes inquiries and discovers that Heinz has led an exemplary life. Role play the two halves of the judge, one wanting to bring Heinz back to

jail, the other wanting to let him go. Or role play Heinz and the judge.

The Faith Healers[2]

In a small Midwestern town, a certain boy of ten has been for several years afflicted with diabetes. The disease is controlled, however, by a daily shot of insulin which keeps the boy in a relatively healthy state. The boy's parents are members of a small religious sect that believes in faith healing. One Sunday they bring the boy to church, where the entire congregation prays for his recovery. At the end of the prayer meeting, the parents announce that the boy has been healed. They throw away his insulin. During the following week, the boy becomes sick and grows progressively sicker. He dies the following Sunday.

Role play a lawyer representing the boy's parents and a lawyer representing the State.

Joe's Problem[3]

Joe is a thirteen-year-old boy. He wants very much to go to summer camp, but the camp costs forty dollars. His father says that he can go if he saves up the money to pay for the camp himself. Joe works hard delivering papers and doing odd jobs after school and has accumulated fifty dollars a few days before camp starts.

But then Joe's father changes his mind. Some of his friends are going on a special hunting trip and he wants to go too, but he doesn't have quite enough money. The father tells Joe that he will have to give up the money he has saved. Joe wants to go to camp, and he doesn't want to give his father the money.

Role play the two halves of Joe, one wanting to do what his father wants, the other half wanting to keep the money.

Extensions

1. Joe decides to tell his father that he has made only ten dollars, but that the camp director has said that he could come anyway and pay later. Joe gives the ten dollars to his father and goes off to camp with the rest of the money. His father can't go on the hunting trip. Joe's older brother, Alan, knows that Joe has lied to his father.

2. Role play the two sides of Alan, one wanting to tell his father that Joe lied, the other wanting not to tell.

3. Role play Joe and Alan talking the night before Joe is to leave for camp.

It should be noted that while the situations described above were devised specifically for the purpose of fostering the development of moral reasoning, many of the other situations suggested for role playing in this book may affect the development of moral reasoning as well. To the extent that a role-playing situation engages the student actively in empathizing—that is, seeing a problem from the perspective of a different person—then that role playing will lead the student to take into account the feelings, motivations, and desires of others as he makes his decisions. The student will then be acting on the basis of more complete information about how his act will affect others, and he will be more likely to make a more generally acceptable moral decision.

And this, after all, is the promise of education: to create a society of truly moral men and women. As Dewey has pointed out, all education should be thought of as moral education, and it is the moral obligation of every teacher to supply every possible aid to the fulfilling of this promise.

Footnotes

1. The basic Heinz dilemma was developed by Kohlberg for research purposes.

2. Based on a newspaper report.

3. Based on a dilemma developed by Kohlberg for research purposes.

RECOMMENDED READING

Berne, Eric. *Games People Play*. New York: Grove Press, 1968. A field guide to the role playing of everyday life. An important way of looking at human behavior.

Dreikurs, Rudolph, *et al. Maintaining Sanity in the Classroom: Illustrated Teaching Techniques*. New York: Harper & Row, 1971. An extremely important and useful book for teachers, especially at the elementary level. Dreikurs outlines a democratic approach to teaching and points out why authoritarian methods are bound to fail. Included are many specific examples of how to discipline students without punishment, and how to encourage students without merely rewarding them.

Eiseman, Jeffrey W. *The Deciders*. Menlo Park, Calif.: Institute for Staff Development, 1969. This is an excellent leader's guide to teaching decision making to adolescent groups. Many practical suggestions, from setting up the room to evaluating the program; uses role playing extensively; includes a phonograph record to use in advance of role playing situations.

Ernst, Ken. *Games Students Play (and What To Do About Them.)* Millbrae, Calif.: Celestial Arts Publishing Co., 1972. A guide to the unconscious role playing that goes on in every classroom, with ideas for how to handle it.

Gelatt, H. B., *et al. Decisions and Outcomes: A Leader's Guide.* New York: College Entrance Examination Board, 1973. Although this is a teacher's guide to accompany student workshops, it contains much valuable information on the decision-making process, as well as many activities which are adaptable for role playing.

Hawley, Robert C., and Hawley, Isabel L. *A Handbook of Personal Growth Activities for Classroom Use.* Amherst, Mass.: Education Research Associates, 1972. Ninety-four activities to promote personal and social growth, with a rationale for each. Naturally, I think that this is a super book.

Hawley, Robert C. *Human Values in the Classroom: Teaching for Personal and Social Growth.* Amherst, Mass.: Education Research Associates, 1973. Sets forth a basic approach to teaching and learning based on specific processes—orientation, community building, achievement motivation, fostering open communication, information processing, value exploration, and planning for change.

Moreno, Jacob L. *Psychodrama*. Beacon, N.Y.: Beacon House, 1946. The father of psychodrama's great work. Still a classic.

Perls, Frederick S. *Gestalt-Therapy Verbatim*. Lafayette, Calif.: Real People Press, 1969. Transcripts of tapes by Fritz Perls, the founder of Gestalt Therapy. The most useful statement of what Gestalt is all about.

Pfeiffer, J. William, and Jones, John E. *A Handbook of Structured Experiences for Human Relations Training* (3 vols.). Iowa City: University Associates Press, 1971. Just what the title says—designed for use with adults but some activities can be applied to classroom situations. Many of the activities involve the use of role playing in one form or another.

Raths, Louis E., Harmin, Merrill, & Simon, Sidney B. *Values and Teaching: Working with Values in the Classroom*. Columbus, Ohio: Charles E. Merrill, 1966. This is the original values clarification manual. It contains the rationale and a wealth of useful value-clarifying activities.

Schmuck, Richard A., and Schmuck, Patricia A. *Group Processes in the Classroom*. Dubuque, Iowa: Wm. C. Brown Co., 1971. Recent research and some practical activities to help teachers become more effective facilitators of group processes.

Shaftel, Fannie R., and Shaftel, George. *Role-Playing for Social Values: Decision-Making in the Social Studies.* Englewood Cliffs, N. J.: Prentice-Hall, 1967. A valuable book, especially for social studies teachers in grades five through eight.

Simon, Sidney B., Hawley, Robert C., & Britton, David D. *Composition for Personal Growth: Values Clarification Through Writing.* New York: Hart Publishing Co., 1973. Originally designed for English teachers but easily adaptable by any teacher trying to humanize his or her classroom.

Simon, Sidney B., Howe, Leland, & Kirschenbaum, Howard. *Values Clarification: A Handbook of Practical Strategies.* New York: Hart Publishing Co., 1972. Chock-full of useful value-clarifying techniques.

INDEX